exploring the
world of Leaves

The peacock plant has
become a favorite
ornamental house plant
because of its beautifully
patterned leaves.

exploring the world of Leaves

Raymond A. Wohlrabe

photographs by the author
diagrams by John F. McTarsney

Thomas Y. Crowell Company
New York

The credits for those photographs not taken
by the author can be found on page 141.

Library of Congress Cataloging in Publication Data

Wohlrabe, Raymond A.
Exploring the world of leaves.

SUMMARY: An introduction to the many different kinds of leaves,
their structure, functions, and importance to plant and animal life. Includes
suggestions for experiments and science projects involving leaves.
1. Leaves—Juvenile literature. [1. Leaves]
I. McTarsney, John F. II. Title.
QK649.W6   581.4'97   75-15865
ISBN 0-690-00511-3

1 2 3 4 5 6 7 8 9 10

acknowledgments

Grateful acknowledgment is made to the scientists who have generously provided information pertaining to their research and discoveries about the leaf and the solutions of some of the problems the normal functioning of leaves have created for man.

The many excellent suggestions that have been offered by the editors who have worked with me in the preparation of this book for publication has been greatly appreciated. Many thanks especially to Ann K. Beneduce and Virginia Buckley of Thomas Y. Crowell Company for their help and encouragement.

The keen interest of many of the young people in plant life and the ways of nature who have been students in my science classes over the years has been a stimulating factor in writing EXPLORING THE WORLD OF LEAVES. They also deserve my appreciation.

Raymond A. Wohlrabe

contents

the fascinating world of leaves 1

Perhaps you have rested in the shade of a tree on a hot summer day and looked up at the pattern of leaves above you. You enjoyed the shade and the relief it offered from the heat of the sun. What you may not have realized is that complex chemical changes were taking place within the sun-dappled leaves above your head. Although you could not see what was happening, each leaf was carrying on work vital to your existence. In fact, life as we know it would not exist on our planet if there were no green leaves. We are directly or indirectly dependent upon them for energy and some of the oxygen we breathe. About three-fourths of the oxygen in the atmosphere comes from the same kind of chemical activity in the algae that thrive in the ocean.

A leaf usually consists of a thin green *blade,* a stalk called a *petiole* that anchors it to a stem or twig, and, at the base of the petiole, tiny leaflike appendages known as *stipules*. Botanists recognize these as the three major parts. The leaves of different species of plants vary widely in shape and appearance. In some kinds of plants, such as the geranium, lilac, or oak, leaf blades are broad; in grasses, the iris, and many others, they are long and narrow. Stipules are often inconspicuous among trees and

In the nasturtium the petiole is attached toward the center of the underside of the leaf and not to the edge of the leaf. For this reason its leaves are said to be *peltate*.

shrubs, although there are herbaceous plants like garden peas in which they grow so large they are easily mistaken for leaf blades. Leaves without petioles are *sessile*.

Two large groupings of trees predominate in North America —the broad-leaf trees and conifers. Among the former are such species as the maple and alder with simple leaves having a single flat blade and others with compound leaves like those of the horse chestnut and the mountain ash with blades consisting of a number of leaflets. In our northern temperate regions most species of broad-leaf trees lose all of their foliage with the approach of winter. These are called *deciduous* trees. Most of the conifers, such as the pines and firs with foliage consisting of needles and the cedars and junipers with overlapping scales, are not deciduous. They are commonly called evergreens. The larches, however, are one of the few conifers that are deciduous.

Nature designs leaves to survive and function under a wide range of conditions that may prevail where they grow. Leaves of trees and shrubs must be able to cope with seasonal and day-to-day changes in their environment from the time they are part of a dormant winter bud until the autumn when they are released from the twigs and flutter to the ground. Laurel and holly leaves have a layer of wax that glosses the surface, reduces the loss of moisture by evaporation, and offers some protection from low temperatures. Some kinds of plants are exposed to long periods of intense sunlight high in the mountains or on the desert floor, where there is little moisture in the atmosphere to filter out sun's rays that harm living cells by overheating them. Many species have leaves covered with silky or woolly hairs to scatter these rays before they can reach sensitive tissues.

Nature has provided other plants with leaves that offer protection from other hazards. If your hand brushes against nettles flanking a woodland trail you experience the sting of its leaf hairs. The leaves of many desert plants have a minimum of surface to reduce evaporation of precious water and in some species of cactus the leaves are modified to form spines for defense. Desert animals desperately in need of water are seldom successful in tearing open a cactus to reach the spongy tissue where it is stored when they are confronted by a barrier of spines.

The silver tree (*Leucadendron argenteum*), which is native to South Africa, has clusters of narrow leaves that shimmer like silver in the sunlight. Each leaf is covered with fine silvery hairs that disperse and deflect a part of the rays of intense sunlight.

Plants of the Arizona
desert like the giant
saguaro and the
spindly-stemmed ocotillo
have leaves modified to
serve as organs of defense.
The process of
photosynthesis is left to
the green tissues of the
stem in the giant saguaro.

Equally as interesting as observing the kinds of leaves among the trees of a forest or in a city park is the fun of discovering extremely modified types that prove how skillfully nature can tailor leaves to meet unusual needs. You will find some examples of these in your own backyard, a garden plot, or among the produce on display in a supermarket. The onion is one of them. Its tubular leaves are green aboveground and white below the surface of the soil. A bulb is formed, built of the concentric layers of the flared-out leaf bases that are telescoped over one another just above the roots of the plant. Carbohydrates (sugars and starches) are stored in the bulb. During the long days of summer, as more and more food produced in the green tissues is stored, the leaf bases thicken and the bulb which we know as the onion grows larger. In some species bulb growth is most rapid when the daylight period extends over twelve to thirteen hours. Then food-making is at its peak in the upper part of the leaves. Farmers who wish to market large dry onions let the plants grow until the bulb has reached its maximum size and the green parts of the leaves have withered and dried. The hyacinth is another plant which produces bulbs built of overlapping leaf bases.

A bract is a type of modified leaf. It is usually scalelike or is some color that contrasts sharply with the green of ordinary leaves. Bracts commonly grow at the base of flowers or the buds of a plant. The white or pink "petals" of the dogwood, a tree or shrub which is native to many parts of North America, are bracts. The dogwood blossom is a composite flower consisting of a large number of inconspicuous yellowish-green flowers clustered so close together they form a button surrounded by four to six large white or pink bracts. These make the flower cluster more conspicuous so as to attract more insects and thus increase the probability of pollination. The poinsettia has bracts for the same purpose. Its tiny blossoms, clustered less compactly than those of the dogwood, are surrounded by large red, white, or pink bracts. The scales so commonly found on leaf buds are also bracts. They are usually stiff and, in some species like the

The white "petals" of the dogwood around the clusters of tiny inconspicuous flowers are modified leaves. They are called bracts.

chestnut, are sticky. They protect the tender bud from cold, insects, and fungi.

You will find some plants with modified leaf parts that bear little or no resemblance to the usual form. In both sweet peas and garden peas, the leaflets of their compound leaves are greatly modified to form tendrils that cling to objects as the plant grows in height. Tendrils are extremely sensitive to contact. When they touch a wire, string, or pole they immediately start to coil around it. There are other plants, which do not belong to the pea family, that have tendrils which are modified stems.

The poinsettia has green leaves and, around its clusters of small inconspicuous blossoms, bright red bracts which are modified leaves. Some varieties have bracts that are pink or white.

These leaves are arranged alternately on the stem and each has pinnately netted-venation.

In some plants the petiole, although not strictly modified, is developed to function in a way other than the normal one of linking the leaf blade to a stem. The petiole of the rhubarb is large with considerable red pigment in its tissues when it is mature. It is a storage place for the sugars and starches manufactured in the leaf. Celery, with diminutive blades and relatively enormous petioles, is another example of a leaf developed with a petiole for storing food.

Light is so vital a source of energy for plants that nature has devised ways of making certain that most leaves get their share of sunlight. They are arranged on stems and twigs to prevent, as far as possible, the complete shading of one leaf by another. The leaves are attached to twigs at points called *nodes* according to patterns determined by the species or family to which the plant belongs. These patterns are very noticeable in the broad-leaf trees. In one such pattern, known as the *opposite arrangement,* one leaf is attached at a node directly across the stem from another, as in the maple. Foliage of the beech and alder have the simplest type of *alternate arrangement,* with a single leaf attached to one node followed down the stem by another on the opposite side. (Botanists now include in this type of arrangement the kind they once classed as spiral.) When three or more leaves are attached to each node, the pattern is said to be *whorled.* Once you have examined the twigs of a few different kinds of trees or shrubs these patterns will become very familiar to you. Petioles of certain species of shrubs and herbaceous plants vary considerably in length in order to bring individual leaves into the light. This creates what is called a leaf *mosaic,* a pattern in a mass of foliage. Excellent examples of this can be seen in the hydrangea, nasturtium, and ivy.

Scientific terms are used to describe some of the characteristics of leaves. These are not difficult, particularly if their meaning is clearly understood. Start with *palmately* and *pinnately*. Both of these terms help scientists to identify the arrangement of leaflets on the petiole of a compound leaf. Examine a lupine in a flower garden or one of the many varieties that grow wild in most parts of North America. Each leaf consists of from seven to eleven lance-shaped leaflets attached to the tip of a long petiole. The lupine leaf is palmately compound, which means that it is shaped like a hand with fingers outspread. The rubber tree, native to the rain forests of tropical lands, also has palmately compound leaves. Each leaf has three elliptically shaped leaflets that are so large they look like individual leaf blades. The upper

This is a good example of a leaf mosaic. The hydrangea leaves are arranged so that as many as possible receive as much light as possible without overshadowing the others.

surface of each of its leaflets is depressed along the midvein to form a trough so that water which would otherwise accumulate on its surface during heavy tropical rains will quickly drain away. Pinnately compound leaves are those in which the leaflets are attached along either side of a central axis which is known as a *rachis*. Pinnate, which means featherlike, is an excellent

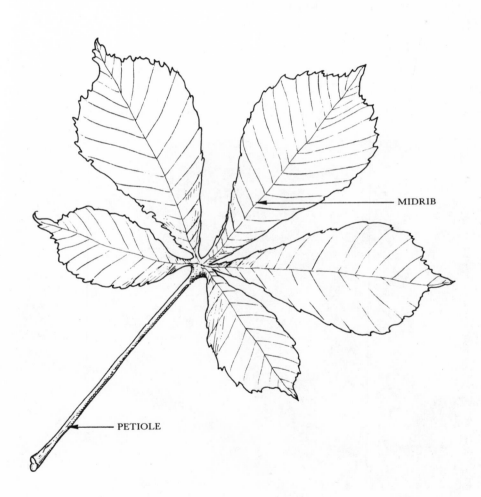

MIDRIB

PETIOLE

The horse chestnut leaf is a palmately compound leaf. It has five or seven leaflets, depending on the species.

word for describing this pattern. The sumac and ash have pinnately compound leaves with up to thirty leaflets attached to the central axis of each.

These terms are also used to identify two of the common types of *venation,* the arrangement of the veins of the leaf blade. Palmately netted-veined leaves have the major veins arranged

The fan palm has a palmately compound leaf. In each the 50 or 60 segments are attached to a strong, stiff petiole bearing spines. Each leaf segment has fiberlike threads along its margin. Two or three species of the fan palm are common in the American Southwest.

like the fingers on the hand; whereas in pinnately netted-veined leaves the veins branch from the midvein like the barbs on the shaft of a feather. Leaves of the maple and the geranium have the former type; those of the alder and cherry, the latter. In both there is a mesh of small veins in the areas between the large veins which, in many species, can be seen by holding the

The leaves of the India rubber tree *(Ficus elastica)* are designed by nature for functioning in the dim light and wet atmosphere of the jungle. They are leathery leaves with large dark-green leaf blades and are shaped to promote the rapid draining of water that might otherwise cling to the leaf surface.

leaf against a strong light. There is also a third type of venation with all of the veins more or less parallel and extending from the base to the tip of the blade, as in the bamboo, corn plant, iris, and lily of the valley. These leaves are parallel veined.

Mention has been made of the ways in which leaf hairs might be of service to a plant. Some sting, some scatter harmful rays in

The dumb cane has large thick leaves with the midrib forming a trough down which rainwater can drain. It grows only in tropical and semitropical lands such as Africa.

light, and some attract insects by secreting a fragrant oil. Plants which are members of the mint family have fragrant leaves, as do catnip, pennyroyal, and thyme. Several species of geranium also have this characteristic. One kind has leaves with the scent of lemon and another a pleasing mint odor. The variety with hairs secreting a scented oil that smells of apples is called the apple geranium. A couple of generations ago housewives added a leaf of the rose geranium to each glass when they made apple jelly to give it an extra-pleasant odor. For many years the oil distilled from wintergreen leaves was used in candy-making until a synthetic substance which duplicates its scent and flavor was developed by chemists and reduced the demand for the more costly natural oil. Either of two methods are commonly used for extracting aromatic oils from leaves. Since some oils are complex organic compounds easily decomposed at temperatures around the boiling point of water, they must be extracted with solvents. For oils not affected by moderate increases in temperature, steam distillation is used.

If you live in a region where mint is grown or the wintergreen plant is found in the ground cover of neighboring woods, steam distillation of leaf oils can be an interesting school or home project. The school science laboratory, however, is the most convenient place to do this experiment. The accompanying diagram will help in setting up the few pieces of equipment that will be needed. Two 250-milliliter Pyrex flasks of either the Erlenmeyer or Florence type must be used. Pyrex glass is important, since the flasks will be heated. Fit one flask with a one-hole stopper, the other with a two-hole stopper. The stoppers must be of some material other than rubber to prevent the distillate from having an unnatural odor. Likewise plastic or glass tubing should be used where tubing is required. The

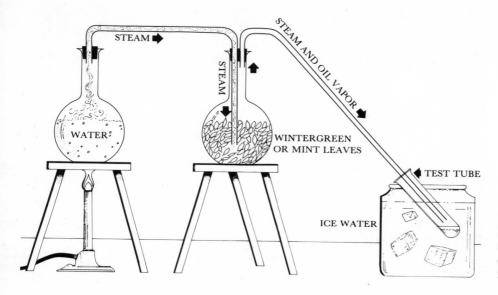

STEAM ➡

STEAM

STEAM AND OIL VAPOR

WATER

WINTERGREEN
OR MINT LEAVES

TEST TUBE

ICE WATER

Diagram of the
apparatus used in
distilling a volatile oil
from leaves.

source of heat can be either an alcohol lamp or a Bunsen
burner. The flask with the one-hole stopper which serves as the
steam generator should be about a third full of water and a tube
must lead from it to the flask with the two-hole stopper filled
about two-thirds full of chopped mint or wintergreen leaves.
Make certain all the tubes fit snugly to prevent leaks. Fit a tube
about a foot and a half long into the other hole of this stopper
and lead it into a large open test tube placed in a larger
container about half full of cold water. *It is very important that this
test tube be left open. Otherwise steam pressure will build up when the
water in the generator is heated.* When the distillation apparatus is
completed, heat the water in the generator to boiling. Steam
will flow into the chopped leaves in the second flask and
vaporize the oil. Continue heating and a mixture of steam and
oil vapor will reach the test tube, condense, and form two layers
of liquid—one of water and the other of fragrant oil.

These leaves show clearly the pattern formed by the large veins in pinnately netted-veining. The venation of the leaves of many broad-leaved angiosperms is of this type.

The bursting of leaf buds after the first sunny days of spring is always a welcome sign that winter is over. It is caused by the rapid growth of tender young leaves that have been dormant all winter. The chestnut tree provides a very dramatic display of this phenomenon. Its buds are several times as large as the buds of most of our common shade trees. Each consists of a cluster of

undeveloped leaves covered by a number of leathery brown
bracts plus the additional protection of a coating of sticky
varnishlike secretion. With the absorption of the warmth of
spring sunshine, sap begins to flow freely in branches and twigs,
the young leaves grow, and the scaly bracts are pushed apart.
Slice a winter bud from tip to base with a razor blade. The
longitudinal section will reveal the undeveloped leaves. A
section cut through a head of cabbage or a Brussels sprout, both
of which are buds, will show a similar pattern.

While you are searching for leaf buds during the winter
months take note of the leaf scars located just below them. The
kind you find on one species of tree will differ from those you
find on other species. These scars are formed in autumn when
the ties that hold the leaves on the twigs are weakened and
suddenly broken by strong gusts of wind. A number of distinct
dots can be seen on each scar. These mark the ends of ducts or

A longitudinal section of
the heads of two different
varieties of cabbage
shows the characteristic
arrangement of the
leaves. A head of cabbage
is a terminal bud.

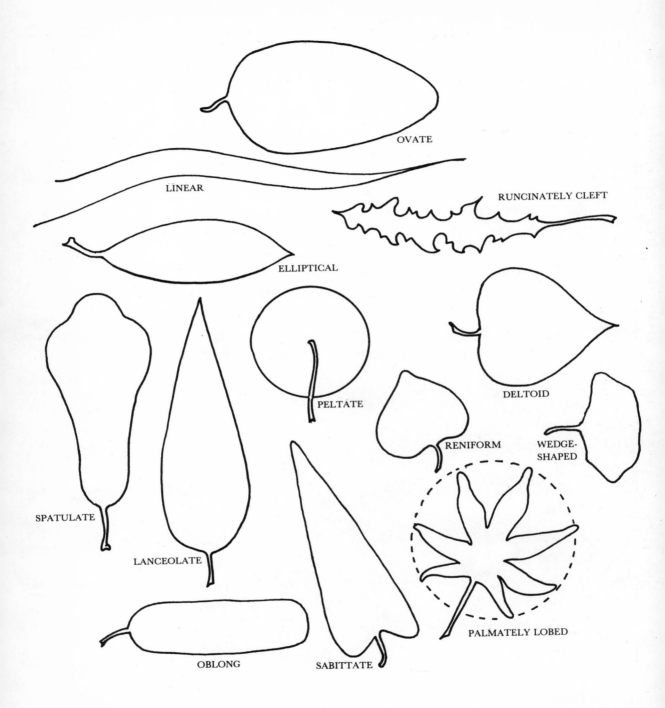

OVATE

LINEAR

RUNCINATELY CLEFT

ELLIPTICAL

PELTATE

DELTOID

RENIFORM

WEDGE-
SHAPED

SPATULATE

LANCEOLATE

PALMATELY LOBED

OBLONG

SABITTATE

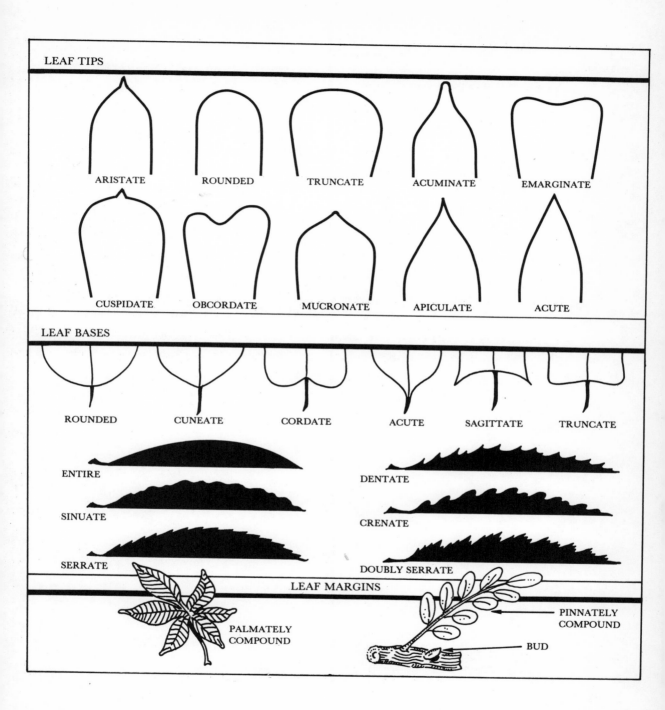

LEAF TIPS

ARISTATE   ROUNDED   TRUNCATE   ACUMINATE   EMARGINATE

CUSPIDATE   OBCORDATE   MUCRONATE   APICULATE   ACUTE

LEAF BASES

ROUNDED   CUNEATE   CORDATE   ACUTE   SAGITTATE   TRUNCATE

ENTIRE   DENTATE

SINUATE   CRENATE

SERRATE   DOUBLY SERRATE

LEAF MARGINS

PALMATELY COMPOUND

PINNATELY COMPOUND

BUD

vascular bundles that linked the petiole to the twig and they are arranged according to a pattern which is characteristic of the species. Ability to recognize these differences can be a help in tree identification.

Interest in leaves usually leads to a desire to identify plants, at least to know to what families or large groups in the plant kingdom they belong. Leaf characteristics play a major role in plant identification. Common terms are frequently used to describe the shape, venation, margin, and the form of the tip and the base of the blade. It will not be difficult to become familiar with the few scientific terms that are used. The preceding leaf charts will help if you check a specimen against the diagrams. When you can recognize the kinds of trees flanking a woodland trail, the shrubs fringing a wilderness lake, and some of the small plants of the ground cover the plant world becomes even more fascinating. Leaves provide clues to climate, soil, hazards—in fact to the whole environment.

inside the leaf 2

Man had to discover what was inside a leaf before he could understand the extraordinary role that green plants play in our lives. Once he learned that small pieces of glass, accurately ground for the proper curvature of surface, could reveal much that is invisible to the human eye, man was well on his way to uncovering the work of green leaves. Although the ancient Greeks knew that glass could be shaped to magnify, they failed to perfect a lens that was useful in exploring plant tissues. The first microscope, invented in the sixteenth century, was not equal in magnifying power to the least expensive microscopes of today. But it opened vast new fields for research. One of these was the power to explore the microstructure of the leaf. In 1590 Jans and Zacharias Janssen, who made eyeglasses for the wealthy burghers of Middleburg in the Netherlands, invented the compound microscope. Less than a century later the Dutch cloth merchant Anton van Leeuwenhoek (1632–1723), who lived in Delft, was examining small insects, discovering hundreds of microorganisms in the water of the canals surrounding the polderlands (lowlands), and becoming famous because of his talent for grinding lenses. He spent every spare moment working at his hobby. His microscopes were single-lensed, but so fascinating was the microworld they revealed that word of the Dutch merchant's hobby spread throughout Europe. Kings, princes, and men of science came to his laboratory in Delft just to have a look through his magic lenses. Leeuwenhoek also wrote letters about what he saw. The Royal Society in London had his writings translated into English and Latin so that those who could not read Dutch might profit by his discoveries.

Others living in this period made improvements in the microscope. One was Robert Hooke (1635–1703), an English physicist, who built compound microscopes, some with three lenses. He focused upon many things, including leaves and stems, and wrote about what he saw in his book *The Micrographia*, published in 1665. Hooke is credited with being the first to use the term *cell* for the tiny units of which both plant and animal bodies are built. A cell, as he described it, was a small compartment bounded by walls. He also observed that cells were filled with juices, but made no mention of it in his writings. Among his excellent drawings that illustrated his writings were sketches of the cells in a piece of cork and of the stinging leaf hairs of the nettle. Nehemiah Grew (1641–1721) was another pioneer microscopist who explored the anatomy of plants and the cellular structure of their tissues. It was being learned that a cell was a far more important and complicated unit than Hooke had thought.

The *nucleus,* which is the center of cell activity, and *protoplasm,* the streaming strands of living substance around it, were discovered. Ellipsoidal or disklike bodies within the protoplasm came into focus as microscopes were improved. These are the *plastids*, of which there are many kinds, each serving the organism of which the cell is a part.

The first microscopes provided man with the means of probing into a world he had never known, and yet there was a limit to what could be seen through them. They created an enlarged image of what lay beneath their lenses by focusing reflected rays of light. However, there are many particles within a cell much too small to reflect light rays, so they remained invisible. These ultramicroscopic particles could not be discovered until some other type of instrument was invented. This problem was solved in the 1930s, when new tools for research were built. These included the electron microscope, which relies upon beams of electrons, instead of light rays, brought into focus by a number of magnetic fields instead of lenses.

There are many different kinds of cells in both plant and animal bodies. When cells having essentially the same structure are grouped together to serve a specific purpose they form a larger structural unit called a *tissue*. A leaf consists of several kinds of tissues. One is the *epidermis*—the outermost layer of cells. It protects the more delicate tissues in the leaf from excessive loss of moisture; from fungus plants like molds, mildews, and bacteria; and from chemical and physical irritation. The epidermis is usually coated with a layer of wax called the *cuticle*. The kind of environment in which the plant lives determines the thickness of this coating. Where there is plenty of moisture it is usually thin; in an arid environment it must be relatively thick. In some plants a thin coating of a resin also covers the epidermis.

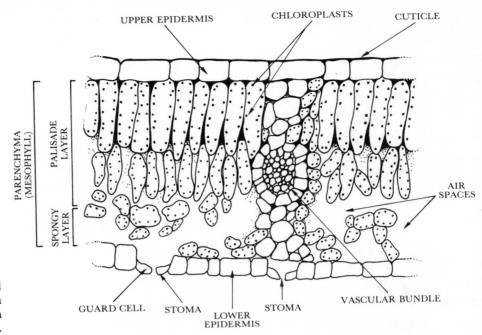

UPPER EPIDERMIS   CHLOROPLASTS   CUTICLE

PARENCHYMA (MESOPHYLL)

PALISADE LAYER

SPONGY LAYER

AIR SPACES

GUARD CELL   STOMA   STOMA   VASCULAR BUNDLE

LOWER EPIDERMIS

Diagram of a typical green leaf as seen in longitudinal section under the microscope.

There are several structural parts that can be considered common to all cells. Each plant cell has an outer wall of cellulose, a nonliving material, which is not found in the cells of animal bodies. It provides protection and support. Cells in animal bodies do not need such support because the tissues of which they are a part are attached to either an internal or external skeleton. Cellulose is a tough substance built of bundles of fibers consisting of long giant molecules.

The wall of a plant cell is not the only means of giving a plant body and its parts a definite form. The amount of fluid in each cell provides rigidity. When the water content of the cells in a plant drops below normal the condition is very noticeable in the leaves. They begin to wilt. The inner surface of the cell

wall is lined with a thin membrane which covers a layer of
protoplasm. Strands of protoplasm lead from this membrane to
the interior of the cell. The membrane is called the plasma
membrane and is selectively permeable, which means that large
particles or molecules in solution cannot pass through it in
either direction, whereas water molecules, dissolved oxygen,
carbon dioxide in solution, and the small molecules of required
nutrients can find their way into the cell. *Cell sap,* a fluid that
carries many of the substances needed to keep protoplasm alive,
fills the pockets, or *vacuoles.* The nucleus, the control center of
the cell, is a small compact body of denser protoplasm
embedded in either the layer of living material just inside the
cell wall or in its strands. It contains still smaller dense bodies
known as *nucleoli* that are thought to have a major role in the
synthesis of protein. Little is known definitely about them. Most
of these parts can be seen through an ordinary low-power
compound microscope.

Epidermal cells are the least complex to be found in a leaf.
Not all of them are alike; a few might be modified. The best
source of epidermis for microscopic examination is the thin
tissue which consists of a single layer of cells lying between the
layers of an onion. From a cut section of an onion separate two
of the layers, tear off a very small piece of this tissue, and spread
it in a drop of water on a clean microscope slide. Since the
nucleus and the protoplasm around it (the *cytoplasm*) are
colorless and not easily distinguished from cell fluids, the piece
of tissue must be stained. At home, tincture of iodine diluted
with rubbing alcohol can be used. In the school science
laboratory, solutions of dyes like fuchsin, methyl violet, or
methylene blue are usually available for staining. Be certain the
specimen is spread without folds or wrinkles in the water on the

slide. Then add a drop or two of the stain, give it a few seconds to be absorbed, and finally press your thumbnail against the edge of the tissue to hold it in place while you rinse away the excess stain with water from a medicine dropper. Put a cover glass on top of the preparation, tap gently with a pencil to work out air bubbles lodged between cover slip and slide, and clamp in position on the stage of the microscope. Adjust the mirror or substage light so the part to be examined can be clearly seen through the eyepiece. By focusing and shifting the slide, center what appears to be the best area in the preparation. With little or no difficulty you will see all the essential parts of the cells with the possible exception of the nucleoli.

Scattered throughout all or part of the epidermis of green leaves are pairs of cells specialized for controlling the tiny pores through which gases are taken into the leaf and water vapor is given off. These are the kidney-shaped *guard cells*. The pore they control is a *stoma*. Pairs of guard cells can be seen clearly with a low-power microscope. Few, if any, guard cells are in the upper epidermis of the leaves of many plants, since stomata in such a position would become clogged with dust particles and dirt brought down with rain. There is an abundance of them in the lower epidermis. It has been estimated that a square centimeter of the undersurface of a leaf of an apple tree has nearly 30,000 stomata in its epidermis, while the upper surface has none. The leaves of some plants, like the geranium, have stomata in the epidermis of both sides, but there are four or five times as many in the undersurface as in the upper. Tear a geranium leaf to expose the colorless epidermis along the torn edge. Remove a small piece, stain it in the usual way, and examine under the microscope. The epidermal cells are arranged like the parts of a jigsaw puzzle. Focus sharply upon the guard cells and you

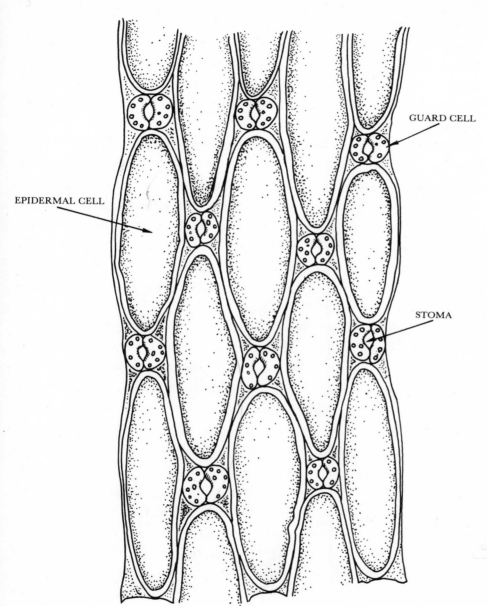

GUARD CELL

EPIDERMAL CELL

STOMA

Cells of the epidermis of an iris leaf showing the pattern of ordinary epidermal cells and the stomata with their guard cells.

might be able to see a few small green dots. These are chloroplasts, the tiny egg-shaped bodies containing the green pigments called chlorophyll *a* and chlorophyll *b,* and will be found in no other cells of the epidermis. By losing water, guard cells shrink and close the stoma; by absorbing it they swell, become more curved on their inner surface, and open the stoma.

The patterns of epidermal and guard cells in different species are rarely exactly the same. In the iris, and in most plants with leaves held in a more or less erect position, stomata are plentiful on both sides. When viewed under the microscope, the regular epidermal cells appear diamond-shaped, with a stoma and a pair of guard cells at each end. Water lily leaves have an entirely different distribution of guard cells and stomata because of the environment in which they live. By far the greater number are in the upper epidermis, which is in contact with air, and relatively few are found on the undersurface of the leaf, which rests on the water.

Between the upper and lower epidermis of the leaves of plants like the geranium, pea, alder, and oak are tissues built of cells containing chloroplasts. This is the mesophyll or green parenchyma, tissues consisting of palisade and spongy layers. The palisade layer is usually built of cylindrical cells partially separated by small air spaces and lying just below the upper epidermis of the leaf. Below it lies the spongy layer consisting of larger cells, irregular in shape, with large air spaces between them. Both layers are green because of the abundance of chloroplasts in their cells. Most of the carbon dioxide and oxygen entering through the stomata dissolves in fluids coating the surface of the cells of the spongy layer and is absorbed. Threading through the mesophyll tissue is a network of veins

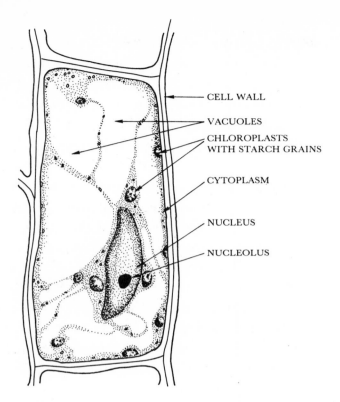

CELL WALL

VACUOLES

CHLOROPLASTS
WITH STARCH GRAINS

CYTOPLASM

NUCLEUS

NUCLEOLUS

Microview of a typical
cell of the mesophyll
tissue showing its
principal parts.

(vascular tissue) which transfers water with dissolved sugars, proteins, and other nutrients to all parts of the leaf or the plant.

It is difficult to prepare a slide that will show the layers of the mesophyll clearly in a cross section unless one has had some experience in shaving a thin slice of a fairly thick leaf with a razor blade. If you wish to try, use a single-edged blade. It should be held firmly to yield a slice that is thin but of uniform thickness. Do not try to cut a section across a leaf by pressing down with the razor blade while the specimen lies flat on a hard surface. The leaf must be placed in an upright position and sliced in much the same way you would slice an apple.

Elodea is an excellent plant to examine microscopically for cells with chloroplasts. There are several varieties; they grow in ponds of stagnant water, along the margins of lakes, and in roadside ditches. It can also be purchased at any store where aquarium supplies are sold. Pluck the smallest leaf you can find from a sprig of elodea, mount it in a couple of drops of water on a slide, and add a cover glass. Staining is not necessary. Focus under bright light and the cells of the leaf will show clearly. Under high magnification the individual bright green chloroplasts can be seen. In bright light you might see them streaming from one end of each cell to the other. They are the plastids in which food is being manufactured. The chlorophyll *a* they hold has an important role in converting water and carbon dioxide to sugar.

It is helpful to know the microstructure of a leaf and become familiar with the parts of a cell in exploring the world of leaves. Some knowledge of this will help one to understand why leaves are designed as they are and how they function as they do. If a microscope is available it can provide a lot of interesting fun.

green magic 3

Photosynthesis, which means putting together by the action of light, is the process by which plants make food from raw materials, using light as the source of energy. With captured bundles of energy called photons, and the carbon dioxide and water absorbed by the plant, sugars and starches are made. It is in the labyrinth of a leaf's highly specialized tissues that this extraordinary process takes place. Scientists have discovered many of the details of this complex procedure but some of the process is still unknown.

Only in recent centuries did man become aware of the process of photosynthesis. It was impossible to understand its nature before carbon dioxide and oxygen were discovered. Some knowledge of it and the role of chlorophyll and light came from clues observed in the seventeenth and eighteenth centuries, but not until the last few decades has research revealed the major details.

Aristotle's explanation of plant growth was generally accepted in ancient times and throughout the Middle Ages. That great philosopher, whose theories remained unchallenged for several centuries, thought that all plants absorbed food through their roots directly from the humus in the soil. One of the first men of science to question this theory was Jan Baptista van Helmont (1577–1644). He weighed a willow sapling and planted it in a pot filled with dry soil which he had also weighed. The willow was then permitted to grow over a period of several years while nothing but rainwater was added to the soil. At the end of this period the tree was carefully uprooted, the soil dried, and each was weighed. The soil had increased in weight merely a fraction of a pound. The tree had gained more than 160 pounds. From these results he concluded that the increase in the weight of the tree was due to the rainwater it had absorbed. Some years later more clues about the growth of plants and the role of the leaf were discovered. Marcel Malpighi (1628–1694), an Italian scientist, was convinced by the results of his experiments that the food a plant requires for growth is manufactured primarily in its leaves.

The discovery of oxygen by Joseph Priestley (1733–1804) in 1774 spurred further research. Priestley was an English clergyman who was interested in scientific investigation, particularly in the field of gases or "airs" as they were called in his time. Shortly before his discovery of oxygen Priestley had demonstrated that plants give off during periods of daylight a gas which animals need in order to live. From previous experiments he knew that a mouse imprisoned in a jar of carbon dioxide suffocated quickly. To his amazement he found that a sprig of mint left standing in a glass of water under a container full of carbon dioxide for about ten days brought about a remarkable change. The green mint leaves did something to the carbon dioxide. He repeated the experiment again and again. Each time the "air" which had suffocated mice before was somehow converted to an "air" that would support life. This puzzled Priestley, so he tried the experiment using sprigs from plants other than mint. One which proved unusually effective in removing the carbon dioxide and replacing it with a gas that sustained life (oxygen) was a sprig of spinach. The conclusion he drew from these experiments was that plants play a part in supplying the atmosphere with the kind of "air" all living things need in order to survive. What he actually proved was that green plants use carbon dioxide in making sugars and in the process give off oxygen as a by-product. In a later experiment Priestley heated the red oxide of mercury, a poisonous substance, by focusing the sun's rays upon it with a burning glass. The "air" he obtained was quite different from the ordinary air of the atmosphere. A lighted candle lowered into a bottle of the gas burned more vigorously with a bright flame. Priestley called it "dephlogisticated air" in his report to the Royal Society in London.

The observations of these men encouraged others to explore. In 1779 Jan Ingenhousz (1730–1799) discovered that green plants exposed to sunlight remove carbon dioxide from air and give off oxygen. He also found that in periods of darkness this activity stops. Four years later the Swiss scientist Nicolas Theodore de Saussure (1767–1843) found that the increase in the weight of a growing plant was at least due in part to the carbon dioxide absorbed by its leaves. Near the end of the eighteenth century, another Swiss, Jean Senebier, proved that green leaves require carbon dioxide for manufacturing food. In 1817 J. Pelletier (1788–1842) and J. B. Caventou (1795–1876) extracted the green pigments from leaves and gave them the names by which we know them today. Little by little the basic explanation of photosynthesis evolved. After the time of these early investigators the electron microscope, chemicals tagged with radioactive substances, chromatography, and other tools and techniques were developed that enabled scientists to discover more of the details of the process.

The amount of carbon dioxide in the lower layers of the atmosphere is normally around 0.03 percent. The gas enters the leaf through the stomata and dissolves in the fluids coating the cells of the mesophyll tissues. It has been estimated that the green plants of the earth use almost 700 billion tons of carbon dioxide annually. The supply is constantly being replenished in the atmosphere through respiration in animals and plants, combustion, the weathering of carbonate minerals, and the decay of organic matter in the earth's crust. Without these sources vegetation could not survive.

Photosynthetic processes in most of the land plants are centered in the loosely packed cells of the mesophyll. The cylinder-shaped cells of the palisade layer of the mesophyll are ideal for the purpose. The long axis of each of these cells is at right angles to the surface of the leaf. This provides enough depth in the cell to permit chloroplasts to be carried away from areas within the cell where light is too intense. Also, the end of each palisade cell that lies next to the epidermis has a curved surface that acts somewhat like a lens, and the epidermal cells above them are also slightly curved. Streaming cytoplasm carries many of the chloroplasts into the light-flooded areas within the cell.

Photosynthesis occurs only in cells that contain chloroplasts, whether they are in the leaf, stem, or any other part of the

plant. Recent research has revealed some interesting details
regarding the structure of chloroplasts. Each contains waferlike
bodies known as *grana* stacked together like coins. Each *granum*
carries molecules of chlorophyll *a* and *b*, the major chlorophylls,
and other pigments. They are the vital machinery or the
factories of the sugar-making process.

Electron micrograph of a
chloroplast showing the
grana which carry
chlorophyll *a* and *b* and
other pigments that have
a vital role in
photosynthesis. The
grana are stacked and
appear as dark lines in
the electron micrograph.

When conditions are favorable and light rays penetrate a leaf surface, photons strike electrons in molecules of chlorophyll *a* in the grana. This gives the electrons with which they collide more energy and they move farther away from the nucleus of the atom of which they are a part. This also happens to electrons in other atoms in the chlorophyll molecule and in neighboring molecules. It creates what is called an excited, activated, or energized molecule and can trigger the first step in photosynthesis which is the breaking down of water molecules into hydrogen ions and molecular oxygen. This is called *photolysis*. Except for the small amount that is used by the plant in respiration, most of the oxygen escapes from the leaves through the stomata. Reactions immediately following this initial step use light energy and the energy released by breaking chemical bonds to form molecules of a number of different kinds of unstable substances. One of these is the important coenzyme adenosine triphosphate, commonly known as ATP. It has the role of a bearer of chemical energy. Since all of the chemical changes which lead to the production of ATP must be initiated through the bombardment of pigments such as chlorophyll by photons they are known collectively as light reactions. It is believed the excited molecules of other pigments in the chloroplasts transfer at least some of the energy they acquired by photon bombardment to chlorophyll *a* molecules.

Since intense sunlight can be harmful to chlorophyll, plants have several ways of adjusting their leaves to reduce the amount of light striking them. It is also possible to shift the position of the chloroplasts so that the amount of light that strikes them is either reduced or increased. In brilliant light they can flatten out to become disklike and arrange themselves in the cell so their edges are turned toward the oncoming rays. In dim light they can become almost spherical so more of their surface will be in the path of the rays.

Through research in the last few decades of the nineteenth century the phenomenon of light absorption by the various pigments was explored. T. W. Engelmann (1843–1909), a pioneer in investigating the relationship between the color of light rays and photosynthetic activity, used an interesting procedure. He used in his research certain kinds of motile bacteria that live in pond water and must have uncombined oxygen gas in order to live. Single filaments of a threadlike green alga abundant in stagnant pools were placed in drops of water well populated by these bacteria on microscope slides in the path of the band of colors of the solar spectrum. In examining these preparations under the microscope Engelmann saw that the bacteria clustered in large numbers around the filament in areas where oxygen was being given off during photosynthesis. The greatest concentration of bacteria was in the area illuminated by the red rays. Smaller swarms formed where the filament was illuminated by blue and violet rays. The amount of oxygen released by the green filament showed considerable variation dependent upon the color of the rays striking it. By counting the bacteria in each area Engelmann was able to make a fairly accurate estimate of the numbers of photons striking in each and conclude under which colors of light photosynthetic activity occurred. Other scientists used other methods to obtain the same information, but most of them were based upon either a direct or indirect determination of the pressure or the volume of oxygen given off under each color of visible light rays. The results showed that green plants absorb photons primarily from the rays of the red and blue-violet bands of the spectrum. There was also evidence that to a much lesser degree photons of the green rays are accepted.

Radiation from the sun includes not only the visible rays but also ultraviolet and infrared rays. The ultraviolet rays have energy capable of breaking the chemical bonds linking together the atoms of molecules. Plant and animal life must be shielded from them. The atmosphere is the shield which nature created to provide this protection—a vast sea of air reaching from the earth's surface to the fringes of outer space. Some of the molecules of its oxygen gas rise toward the upper layers of the atmosphere, are broken down by the action of ultraviolet rays into atoms of oxygen, and then these combine to form ozone, a strong absorber of ultraviolet light. As radiation is transmitted through the atmosphere molecules of carbon dioxide absorb infrared rays and then reradiate them to the earth's surface. This is beneficial to life since the warming effect of infrared prevents the earth's surface temperature from dropping to extremely low levels at night. Water vapor molecules in the air absorb infrared rays as well.

Cloud masses in the atmosphere also reduce markedly the transmission of light rays with a corresponding reduction in photosynthetic activity. Molecules of nitrogen gas and particles of dust have a similar effect as do the substances released as wastes into the upper layers of the atmosphere. Such pollutants become partial barriers to the transmission of solar radiation and create what some scientists call a dirty sky, a condition of great concern to many because particles reaching high levels in the stratosphere do not settle. Accumulated particles might eventually absorb enough visible light to have a harmful effect upon the process of photosynthesis in green plants. Environmentalists point to this possibility in their war against dumping wastes in the atmosphere whether from industrial plants or the emissions from supersonic planes.

Scientists have estimated that about half of the sun's rays that strike the upper atmosphere reach the earth's surface. But much of this is reflected from the ground, foliage, and other surfaces so that only a very small fraction of the sun's light rays actually provide energy for photosynthesis.

The 1930s brought a better understanding of the chemistry of photosynthesis. It was discovered that many elements occur in more than one form with the atoms of each having very slight differences in characteristics except for the difference in atomic mass. The various forms are called isotopes. Radioactive isotopes of carbon and oxygen became the "tagged" elements used to probe the complex chemical reactions in the green tissues of plants. Coupled with this was the use of paper chromatography which is a method of separating and identifying substances occurring in solution in extremely small quantities.

Experiments undertaken during this period by Nobel prize-winner Melvin Calvin and his associates at the University of California and by other groups of researchers determined what happens to carbon dioxide in photosynthesis. Certain species of green algae were grown in tanks and allowed to absorb carbon dioxide in which the carbon atoms were the radioactive isotope C^{14}. This variety of carbon emits beta rays as it decomposes which makes it possible to trace the element through the series of intermediate reactions that occur before hexose sugar is formed. The many complex compounds were identified in these step-by-step changes by the technique of paper chromatography and placing the strip of paper in which they were absorbed (the chromatogram) on a photographic paper sensitive to beta rays. Calvin's research revealed that oxygen in the carbon dioxide molecule is not released as oxygen gas. The oxygen given off as a by-product during photosynthesis comes entirely from the water, and the hydrogen ions of water molecules are combined with carbon dioxide molecules to form carbohydrates (sugars

Equipment used by Dr. Calvin in his research on the intermediate chemical reactions of photosynthesis at the University of California.

and starches). Scientists speak of such a change as the reduction GREEN MAGIC
of carbon dioxide by hydrogen ions.

The chemical equation ordinarily used to give the chemistry of photosynthesis is a condensed form and as such gives no clue as to the complex series of reactions which lead to the final products. It is a simple equation, usually written:

$$CO_2 + 2H_2O \rightarrow (CH_2O) + O_2 + H_2O$$

or more realistically:

$$6CO_2 + 12H_2O + \text{light energy} \rightarrow C_6H_{12}O_6 + 6O_2 + 6H_2O$$

But, despite all that has been learned about the intermediate reactions in recent decades, this compact summation of what takes place will continue to be used.

The chemical changes that follow the light reactions can be carried out in the absence of light and are called the *dark* reactions. They must, however, be preceded by light reactions.

A hexose sugar, usually glucose, is the major end product of the complex changes that take place during photosynthesis. Each of the molecules of a hexose sugar has six carbon atoms linked with hydrogen and oxygen atoms. During daylight hours much more sugar is manufactured in the leaves than a plant actually needs. With the help of enzymes in the cell fluids most plants convert the large excess of sugar to starch, a substance which is insoluble in water.

An interesting experiment can be carried out at home if there is tincture of iodine in the medicine cabinet. It will prove that starch is produced in leaves and that light is required to produce the sugar from which starch is formed. Tincture of iodine is an alcoholic solution. When it comes in contact with starch a blue-black coloration appears. The medicinal iodine solution is quite concentrated and should be diluted by adding twice its volume of rubbing alcohol. Remember that *alcohols are inflammable and poisonous. They should never be tasted, their vapors should not be inhaled, and they should not be brought near a flame.* Keep bottles containing such alcoholic solutions out of reach of children.

A potted geranium plant will be needed. Keep it in complete darkness for two days. Then cover one or two of its leaves with aluminum foil to shield them from light that might reach their surface. Do the same with two or three other leaves, using aluminum foil in which a hole about an inch in diameter has been cut. When these are exposed to light, it will permit the light rays to strike only a small area of the leaf surface. When the foil has been carefully adjusted, bring the plant into bright sunlight for a day. Then remove a leaf not covered with foil—one that has been fully exposed to the sun's rays. Put it in rubbing alcohol in an open jar or beaker and place the container in a pan of hot water. Do not try to heat the jar with a flame; it will break and the alcohol will catch on fire. Hot water in the pan, not boiling, will provide a temperature high enough for the alcohol to boil. This, done carefully, will remove most of the green color from the leaf. Then lift the specimen from the alcohol, rinse, and drop into dilute iodine solution. Almost immediately the entire leaf will turn blue-black. Do the same with a leaf that was completely covered with foil. Since it was not exposed to light, no sugar was produced from which a deposit of starch could be formed and little or no blue-black color will be produced. Use the same procedure with one of the leaves exposed to light in only one small area. It will turn blue-black only where light rays struck the leaf surface by passing through the hole cut in the foil. This experiment shows quite clearly that light is required in photosynthesis and that the sugar manufactured is held temporarily in the leaf by being converted to starch.

At night, when the absence of sunlight halts photosynthetic activity, the starch stored in the leaf is converted back to sugar. In solution in the sap it is transported to other parts of the plant, where it is broken down for the release of energy or again changed to starch to provide a stockpile of potential energy.

Sugar produced in the leaf is also used to build molecules of cellulose for making cell walls and fibers or in manufacturing organic acids that are needed in some plant activities. Sugar can also be changed to fats and oils. They can be altered chemically by linking with the nitrogen of ammonium compounds formed from nitrates, and nitrites absorbed from the soil, to yield the amino acids a plant must have to produce proteins for building new protoplasm. Hexose sugars play a major role in the growth and life of a plant.

Basically photosynthesis is a process of storing energy. Then, when energy is needed, molecules of sugar are broken down to release some of the energy that binds together the parts of each molecule and convert it to other forms of energy. This is done in each individual cell through a process called *respiration.*

The chemical equation ordinarily used to summarize respiration is the reverse of the one used for photosynthesis. It is written:

$$C_6H_{12}O_6 + 6O_2 \rightarrow 6CO_2 + 6H_2O + \text{energy}$$

It also is a simple equation that merely summarizes a series of chemical changes which are the same in plants and animals.

The actual seat of respiration lies in each living cell. It is

An osmosis demonstration using materials available around the home. Only the glass tube and a one-hole rubber stopper need be obtained. The cavity in the carrot was made with an apple corer and partially filled with sugar, a little water, and a few drops of red food color before inserting the stopper. Water to near the top of the carrot filled the jar. Within twenty-four hours, the red-colored sugar solution had risen thirteen inches.

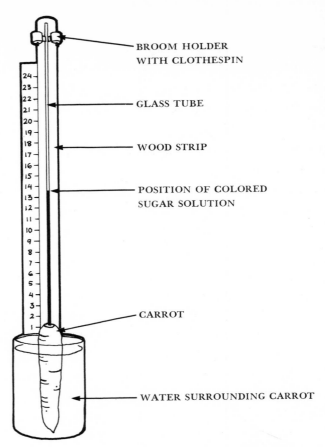

BROOM HOLDER WITH CLOTHESPIN

GLASS TUBE

WOOD STRIP

POSITION OF COLORED SUGAR SOLUTION

CARROT

WATER SURROUNDING CARROT

there that a series of two separate groups of chemical reactions occur. The first group includes those reactions that break down the molecules of sugars or other organic substances in the cell fluids to form substances like organic acids built of smaller, less complex molecules. Citric acid is one of the acids formed. In scientific circles this initial group of reactions constitute what is called *glycolysis*. The second group includes the reactions in which the simple compounds produced during glycolysis are combined with oxygen. This is *oxidation*. In plants and animals it must not be too rapid. Sudden oxidation would cause a considerable loss of energy released as heat and the heat would

damage the cells through injury to the protoplasm. Enzymes
produced in the cells control the speed at which both glycolysis and respiration occur. They are organic catalysts—substances that alter the speed of a chemical change without undergoing a permanent change in their composition. Research since the invention of the electron microscope has revealed the source of the respiratory enzymes. Extremely small particles, or organelles, known as *mitochondria* within each living cell produce these enzymes. They have the power to release energy safely through oxidation and, for this reason, are sometimes called the "power-packs" of living cells.

It is fortunate for man and all other forms of life on the earth that leaves manufacture many times the quantity of sugars plants need to meet their own requirements. The excess is usually deposited as starch, sugar, and other nutrient substances in the tissues of the plant. Part of this stored energy is released through respiration either directly by animals that use plants as food or indirectly by those that feed upon other animals. Man has also found other ways of making use of the energy stored in starches and cellulose. Since his discovery of fire many ages ago he has been burning wood or such fossil fuels as coal and oil to keep him warm or to cook his food. In more recent times he has been using these fuels to operate steam and internal combustion engines and in power plants to generate electricity. Some animals even use this stored energy released as heat during the process of fermentation. An excellent example of an animal that does this is the alligator. It incubates its eggs by piling rotting vegetation on top of them and relying on the heat generated by further decay. Then its only responsibility in bringing young alligators into the world is to guard the nest and protect the young after they hatch.

leaves and the
4 problem of water

Leaves waste most of the water that reaches them from the soil and in doing so they create a problem for man, who must find ways to conserve this precious resource. Plants cannot live without water. The surfaces of the sugar-manufacturing cells must be kept moist. Water carries in solution the carbon dioxide, oxygen, and minerals essential to the life of a plant. It also permits the translocation of food substances made in the leaves to where it is needed or to where it is to be stored. However, plants draw much more water from the soil than they can actually use.

Neil C. Turner, a scientist with the Connecticut Agricultural Experiment Station in New Haven, estimated that the blades of grass in one acre of lawn will convert 27,000 gallons of water taken from the soil to water vapor and pass it on to the surrounding air each week of the summer season. He also claims

the leaves of all the trees in the forests of his state give up a total
of 50 billion gallons of water to the atmosphere in this same
period. J. C. Cummings, another scientist, has determined that
an average-size silver maple 48 to 50 feet tall can release nearly
60 gallons of water an hour as vapor on a summer day. The
energy required to convert water to vapor comes from the
sunlight that penetrates the surface of the leaves. The vapor
escapes through the cuticle, the stomata, and also through the
surface of stems not covered by a heavy bark. The real culprits
causing most of the water loss from plants are the stomata.
Scientists know the loss of water from plants by evaporation as a
process called *transpiration.*

For decades researchers have been trying to find how water
from the soil reaches the leaves of tall trees with their uppermost
branches three or four hundred feet above the forest floor. Most
of it enters the tree through the root hairs on the tips of the
roots. Root hairs are fingerlike projections of the epidermal cells
of the root tip that reach into the spaces between soil particles in
search of water. The soil water carrying dissolved substances
passes through their cell walls, which are built largely of
cellulose fibers embedded in *pectin*, a carbohydrate of jellylike
consistency. The cell wall is completely permeable; it permits
both water and dissolved substances to pass through it. Just
inside the wall is a lining of living cytoplasm enclosed in thin
protoplasmic membranes which are selectively permeable. The
membrane on the inner surface of the lining, called the *tonoplast,*
is in contact with the cell sap, a solution of minerals, sugars, and
several organic substances in water. It is the membrane
primarily concerned with permitting water to enter the root
hair from the soil by a process called *osmosis.*

When water solutions having different concentrations of

molecules are separated by a selectively permeable membrane, osmosis occurs. It can also be described as a flow of water molecules through such a membrane into a solution less concentrated with water molecules. This flow creates osmotic pressure, a force extremely vital in the life processes of both plants and animals. The classic example used to illustrate osmosis is a sugar solution separated from pure water by a membrane with such small pores that sugar molecules, many times larger than those of water, cannot pass through. Water molecules bombard both sides of the membrane and penetrate it in both directions. But in the sugar solution the greater total concentration of molecules creates a "molecular traffic jam" that hinders bombardment of the membrane by water molecules. Sugar molecules get in their way so that fewer of them strike the membrane in a given unit of time as compared with the number which strike on the opposite side of the membrane. Consequently more water flows into the sugar solution than out of it.

Osmosis can be demonstrated either in the school science laboratory or at home. Drill a cylindrical cavity about one and a half inches deep into the stem end of a taproot such as a carrot, turnip, or parsnip. It should be large enough in diameter to let a one-hole soft rubber stopper fit snugly into its upper part. Then fit the end of a transparent plastic tube several feet long into the hole of the stopper. After sugar, a small amount of water, and a few drops of food color have been put in the cavity insert the stopper and make certain it is sealed by smearing melted sealing wax or beeswax over both the top of the root and around the base of the tube. The demonstration will not be successful if sugar solution leaks from the cavity. When the wax has hardened carefully lower the taproot into a jar or beaker and support the plastic tube in an upright position. The tube can be taped to a yardstick held upright by burette clamps on a ring stand if the demonstration is carried out in school. Pour water into the jar to within about a half inch of the top of the root. Within an hour water which has worked its way by osmosis through the cells of the wall of the root will have increased the volume of the sugar solution enough to cause it to rise into the tube. It will continue to rise for a day or two; perhaps to a height of four or five feet. When the hydrostatic pressure due to the weight of the liquid in the tube equals the osmotic pressure, the movement of the sugar solution up the tube will halt. The column of sugar solution that moves up the tube will be clearly visible because of the food color dissolved in it. The demonstration should provide ample proof that the cytoplasmic membranes of the cells of the tissues of the root are selectively permeable. Little or no sugar or food color can be detected in the water in the jar or beaker.

Turgor, a condition vitally important to the normal growth and functioning of plants, is maintained by osmotic pressure. When the volume of sap in the vacuole of a cell increases, the elastic layer of cytoplasm around it with its delicate membranous covering expands. Eventually the cytoplasm pushes hard against the more rigid cell wall and the wall exerts a pressure against it. The inflow of water molecules toward the vacuole slows down and when the wall pressure balances the osmotic pressure, it stops. The cell is then said to be fully turgid. In small plants like the violet and dandelion that do not have stems strengthened by wood fibers the turgor of its cells keeps the stems upright, the leaves in their normal position on the stem, and prevents any parts of the plant from drooping or wilting.

Some decades ago scientists became aware of osmosis and its role in providing water for plants. As water from the soil moves into a cell the sap in the cell vacuoles becomes more dilute. Large numbers of water molecules flow from them to neighboring cells. Likewise water is transferred from one layer of cells to another deeper within the cortex of the root until it eventually reaches the core *(stele)* and diffuses into the xylem. This osmotic activity in the cells that lie between the soil and the ducts of the

Tomato plants have an unusually large number of stomata. They give off enormous amounts of water vapor during transpiration. Both tomato and corn plants have come to be known as the most notorious water wasters.

xylem creates a region surrounding the core of the root that acts somewhat like a single selectively permeable membrane. As the water molecules move inward they are accompanied by the molecules and ions held in solution. Although absorption of water by osmosis is a relatively slow process, it can create very strong pressures. This is easy to understand when we realize how great is the number of tiny root hairs possessed by even the smallest of plants and how enormous is the total surface exposed to soil water.

When water reaches the central core of the root it enters the xylem ducts of the vascular tissue and rises toward the stem through tubes called vessels and tracheids. This upward movement of water creates what is called *root pressure*. Vessels and tracheids are elongated cells. They function only after they have reached maturity and the living substance within them is dead. They have pits where their walls are very thin to permit the transfer of water from one vessel to another in the bundles of which they are a part. In the early periods of their growth the vessels of the xylem consist of short cells stacked above one another. As they mature the wall at either end of each cell where they are in contact with cells above or below them in the stack dissolve and a tube is created.

Another type of tubular cell is found in the phloem (a specialized conducting tissue similar to the xylem) of the stele and the stem. This is the *sieve tube*. These cells are linked end to end and the wall at each end is perforated like a sieve. Each is accompanied by a *companion cell*. Strands of cytoplasm from adjacent cells extend through the perforations of the sieve plates to link each cell with those that are directly above or below it and this facilitates movement of liquids. Sieve tubes serve primarily to transport solutions of sugar and other nutrients downward from the leaves to provide these substances which are needed to meet the food requirements of all parts of the plant.

Years ago it was thought that root pressure alone was responsible for the rise of water in stems. The observation that water exudes from the cut stems of many plants was largely responsible for this theory. Today it is known that root pressure plays only a small part in conducting water through a plant. Other forces are now known to have a major role.

When a tree is just a tiny seedling it has well-developed vascular bundles, and osmotic pressure has created root pressure strong enough to fill its ducts with water in its first growing season. Growth the following summer will bring an increase in the height of the plant and the formation of more vessels and tracheids in the xylem—new ducts that grow from what is called the *cambium layer.* They draw water from the ducts which had been functioning the previous season. The next season's growth will provide more vessels and they will be filled with water in like manner. Year after year this continues and long columns of water are formed that reach to the top of the tree. Cohesion, the force or attraction which tends to attract molecules of the same kind to each other, is now believed to be the force which prevents these long water columns from breaking.

The columns of water in the tubes of the xylem move slowly through the stem toward the leaves at a speed dependent upon the rate at which transpiration occurs. This is called the transpiration flow. The loss of water from the leaves as vapor creates a suction pressure or diffusion pressure deficit (DPD) which tends to produce a tension or upward pull on the molecules in the water columns. The cohesive force holding the water molecules together causes those farther down each column to move up instead of breaking away. The tension becomes apparent in the roots and results in more water being drawn from the soil. The transpiration flow brings water that is needed in photosynthesis to the cells where photosynthetic activity is carried on. The water carries in solution the minerals required by the plant in its manufacture of substances other

The large tender leaves of the sunflower are vulnerable to attacks by insect pests. Also, through excessive loss of water during transpiration or a lack of sufficient water in the soil, they can lose their normal turgidity and wilt.

than carbohydrates. The transpiration flow is controlled more by the guard cells on either side of each tiny stoma on the leaf surface than by any other factor.

Exactly what causes guard cells to open and close the stomata is not completely understood. It is known, however, that changes in the turgor of guard cells brings about changes in

In this sunflower plant conditions are such that the normal turgor is maintained and the leaves have not wilted.

their shape. Their walls are not of uniform thickness. The wall next to the stoma is very thick; that covering the rest of the cell is relatively thin. As water is absorbed by the cell the turgor increases and the cell expands. The thin part of the wall bulges and draws the thicker part which lies opposite toward it. This causes the stoma to become larger and permits air to enter and water vapor to escape from the pockets in the mesophyll tissue. The turgor decreases when water is lost from a guard cell. When this happens guard cells on either side of a stoma come close together and practically close the opening between them.

Various theories have been offered to explain what determines when guard cells become turgid and expand to open a stoma and what determines when they become flabby and close it. A theory quite generally accepted some years ago explained how osmotic pressure in these cells brought about change. Each guard cell has a few chloroplasts, a major distinction between it and other cells of the epidermis of the leaf. Light which strikes the guard cells triggers photosynthethic action and produces molecules of sugar in the cell fluids. This decreases the concentration of water molecules within the cell and causes water from neighboring cells to flow through the membranes of its cytoplasm until it reaches maximum turgidity. The increased pressure upon its walls changes the shape of the guard cell so that the stoma opens. Toward sundown the light reactions of photosynthesis cease, sugar is slowly carried to the fluids in the ducts of the phloem, and the greater flow of water molecules is in the reverse direction, through guard cell membranes. The cells become flaccid and the stoma are at least partially closed. Opponents of this theory, however, argue that the change in shape of the guard cells could not occur quickly enough because the amount of sugar produced by so few chloroplasts would at

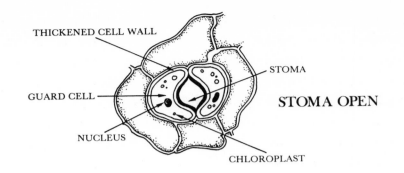

THICKENED CELL WALL

STOMA

GUARD CELL

NUCLEUS

CHLOROPLAST

STOMA OPEN

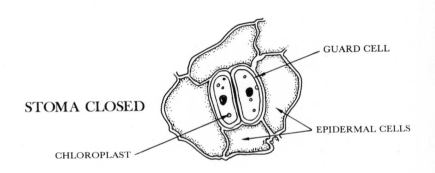

GUARD CELL

STOMA CLOSED

EPIDERMAL CELLS

CHLOROPLAST

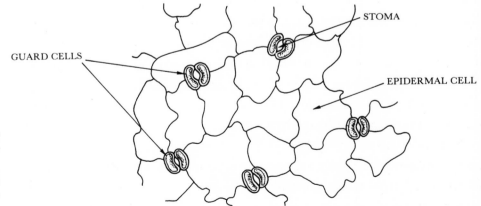

STOMA

GUARD CELLS

EPIDERMAL CELL

The lower epidermis of
the geranium leaf
showing its epidermal
cells and the stomata as
seen under the
microscope.

best create a very weak diffusion pressure deficit. Other theories have been offered but much remains to be learned about this phenomenon before an acceptable explanation can be given.

Stomata vary considerably in size and number in different species of plants. The smallest are about three microns wide and of slightly greater length. The largest are roughly triple the size of the smallest. A micron is a unit of linear measurement used by scientists that is equal to approximately a thousandth of a millimeter. There are 25.4 millimeters in one inch. Scientists have estimated the number of stomata in one square inch of leaf surface to range from around 7,000 in some species to almost 400,000 in others. The leaves of corn and tomato plants have an enormous number of stomata. Both are included among the plants that have a reputation for being the worst wasters of soil water.

The stomata of most plants are open during the daylight hours and closed at night. There are conditions, however, that can cause them to close during the day. This happens when insufficient water is reaching the plant through its root hairs during a period of drought. It can also occur when the temperature of the air is high and the humidity is low. Such conditions would create too rapid a rate of transpiration if the stomata remained open and the plant usually wilts because of an excessive loss of water. Wilting as a rule is first noticeable in the leaves. Providing water for the soil and shade to protect the plant from intense sunlight will bring conditions back to normal and the leaves will lose their limpness.

Nature has also equipped some leaves with the means of combating conditions that are the opposite of those which cause wilting. If the air is extremely humid or the soil is almost saturated with water, transpiration will be reduced. Under

Chlorophyll can be extracted from geranium or spinach leaves by boiling them in rubbing alcohol. A green solution is formed. Since alcohol boils at a lower temperature than water, the glass jar holding the leaves can be placed in near-boiling water in a Pyrex pie plate. This will eliminate any danger of the alcohol igniting. *Do not inhale the vapor.*

these conditions many plants can exude drops of water at leaf margins and tips since they are receiving more than the amount of water they need and the excess cannot be removed by transpiration. At the tip and along the margins of the leaf nature has provided *hydathodes*, a means for relief in such an emergency. These are pores marking the ends of veins. Excess water taken into the plant is forced out through the hydathodes. Under normal conditions they are not used. This phenomenon, in which drops of water appear along the leaf margin and are very noticeable at the leaf tip, is called *guttation*.

The lack of water in the soil in some areas of the United States, particularly in the American Southwest, has led to a lowering of the water table and an increasing need for water from neighboring regions for irrigation. For this reason the control of transpiration to prevent an enormous loss of water from the soil is attracting considerable attention among research scientists.

autumn's carnival of color 5

Autumn brings to the temperate zones of the world a carnival of color unknown in the tropics and other regions. When nature paints the foliage of trees and shrubs with masses of gorgeous color, no man-made spectacle can equal the beauty of her display. It is an unforgettable time, the finale to the warm days of summer. The signal for the change comes when nights get cool. During this prelude to winter one can stroll down a woodland trail under a canopy of gold and flaming red. Fortunate, too, are the motorists who follow the winding roads off the freeways of New England to enjoy the color of sugar maples in autumn. In central Utah, where the Wasatch Mountains meet the farmlands on the fringes of the desert and along the streets of villages tucked between the walls of red rock in the canyons, poplar trees become spindles of gold. The leaves of aspens turn yellow on the high mesas of New Mexico and

Maple leaves turn
brilliant yellow in
autumn.

along the borders of alpine lakes in the Rockies. Nature paints a
masterpiece with the brilliant yellow of the foliage of cottonwood trees against the pastel greens of sagebrush in desert
basins and the purple of distant mountains in Arizona and
Nevada. She bronzes the foliage of sprawling oaks on the
sunburnt Livermore Hills east of San Francisco Bay and
splotches the slopes below the snow line with the yellow of
blueberry bushes on Mount Rainier in Washington State. In

one last splurge before winter she is at work all across America, redecorating on a grand scale. Then, with the exception of the cottonwoods of the Southwest, which have yellow leaves that cling to the branches well into spring, late autumn comes roaring in with gusty winds which bring about an end. Foliage grows thin as leaves flutter to the ground. The carnival is over.

The scientific explanation of what causes this beautiful display of color each autumn is interesting. For centuries it was thought that early frosts were the cause. Science has proven this theory false; a frostbitten leaf does not turn to brilliant yellow, red, or orange. It withers, becomes brown, and falls from the twig. Extensive research has revealed facts about color pigments in the cells of leaf tissues that have become the basis of the modern explanation.

Pigments are located in the grana of plastids distributed through the cytoplasm of mesophyll cells. The grana that carry chlorophyll predominate over those carrying pigments other than green during the summer season. One of the two major kinds of chlorophyll is the bluish-green pigment called chlorophyll a, for which biochemists give the formula $C_{55}H_{72}O_5N_4Mg$. The formula indicates that each molecule is a combination of atoms of each of the elements carbon, hydrogen, oxygen, nitrogen, and magnesium. The number of atoms of each element in the molecule is indicated by the subscript below the symbol of the element. The other kind of chlorophyll, known as chlorophyll b, is a yellowish-green pigment with the formula $C_{55}H_{70}O_6N_4Mg$. This has atoms of the same elements in its molecule, but the number of atoms of oxygen and hydrogen differ. All grana carry other pigments, which are not chlorophylls. These are the xanthophylls, which are yellow-orange, and the carotenes, which are yellow. They are masked during the summer by the green of the chlorophylls. During the cool nights of autumn, when sap flows more slowly in plants, changes occur in the green chlorophyll to cause it to deteriorate rapidly. At that time the leaves become yellow or orange.

Another group of color pigments that appears when cool nights bring changes in the composition of the sap is the anthocyanins. Chemists class them as glucosides, very complex substances built of a combination of colored organic compounds and glucose, a sugar. Anthocyanins are responsible for the reds and purples of autumn leaves. The lower nighttime temperatures and the decrease in the intensity of sunlight in autumn cause an increase in the acid and sugar content of the sap which stimulates the formation of red and purple anthocyanins. Their colors, too, become noticeable when changing conditions destroy the green chlorophyll. A few of the plants that develop brilliant reds in their leaves in autumn are poisonous, like poison sumac. The common sumac is not poisonous. In addition to the poison sumac, which is usually found only in swampy woods, there is a very poisonous member of the sumac family, the poison ivy, which is normally a shrub or vine. Leaf collectors should learn to recognize these plants so they can be avoided. Restrict your autumn leaf-collecting of red leaves to the beautiful specimens that can be found among the maples, woodbine or Virginia creeper, and a host of other nonpoisonous species.

Among the trees that develop an abundance of carotenes and xanthophyll there are some species that also form tannins in their leaves in autumn. The oaks are excellent examples. Tannins tend to create a brown color among the yellow pigments. The concentration of the tannin determines whether a green oak leaf will turn to gold or bronze. Tannin in the sap

The woodbine or Virginia creeper, a member of the grape family, is a vine with compound leaves that turn brilliant red in autumn.

also affects the color of leaves that have a high concentration of the red pigments of the anthocyanin group. Its presence creates a bluish or purplish hue among the reds.

In certain kinds of plants the nature of the sap is such that anthocyanins are developed in the spring the moment the young leaves burst from their buds. These leaves also possess the chlorophylls, but the normal overabundance of anthocyanins masks the green color of these substances. Some varieties of Japanese maple such as *Acer palmatum sanguineum* Lem., *A. p. ornatum* Andre, and *A. p. atrolineare* Schwer. are excellent ex-

The oak leaf is pinnately veined, deeply notched to form an odd number of lobes, and has a shiny upper surface. Tannins affect its color in the autumn.

amples, since their leaves are mostly red or purplish red from spring to autumn. The only noticeable change in their color in autumn is a decrease in the purplish or bluish hue and the resulting intensification of the reds.

All of the color pigments can easily be extracted from leaves. If you wish to try, grind a handful of spinach or parsley leaves to a pulpy mass. It is essential that the leaves be well broken up so the solvent to be used can be easily absorbed. In the school science laboratory this can be done with a mortar and pestle. Add a teaspoon of clean white sand to the crushed leaves to facilitate the grinding. When the material is partially broken up add some alcohol and grind some more. Rubbing alcohol can be used. *Remember that this alcohol is poisonous if it is tasted or if the vapor is inhaled. It is also inflammable.* However, if this is kept in mind and the proper precautions are taken, there is no danger in using it. After thoroughly grinding the mixture, pour the green solution into a funnel holding either a filter paper, some absorbent cotton, or glass wool, and as it flows through, catch it in a glass jar or beaker.

A partial separation of the yellow and green pigments in the solution can be made by paper chromatography. For the best results a wedge-shaped strip of a special type of porous paper called chromatography paper can be used. An inch from the narrow end of the wedge, make a dot by touching it with a toothpick dipped in the solution and letting it dry. Repeat twenty or thirty times until a good deposit of the mixture of pigments is built up, but keep the dot no larger than a quarter of an inch in diameter. Next pour the colorless solvent, rubbing alcohol, to a depth of about half an inch in a clean mayonnaise jar. Fold the wide end of the wedge so that it can be hung from the inside of the cover of the jar with its narrow end dipping slightly into the solvent. Screw the cap on the jar and let it stand undisturbed. As the solvent is absorbed it will move slowly up the strip carrying with it the pigments from the spot of residue. Since chlorophylls are absorbed at a different rate from either the xanthophylls or carotenes, they will separate as they spread upward from the spot on the paper to different heights.

Since the yellow pigments will be carried farther, they will be exposed in a small area above the green due to the chlorophylls. Separation of these pigments can be made in a similar way by folding a white paper napkin to form a narrow cone. Then let the point of the cone dip into the green solution prepared by grinding leaves and immersing them in alcohol. After standing for a few minutes, remove and unfold to examine the napkin. There will be a central disk of green, and, beyond it, a fringing band of yellow.

Near the end of summer the drop in nighttime temperatures brings another change which has its influence on leaves. A layer of cells of the parenchyma tissue normally lies at the base of the petiole where it is in contact with the twig. Enzymes begin dissolving the pectin in these cells. Slowly this layer, known as the *abscission layer,* disintegrates. Eventually all that remains to attach the leaf stalk to the twig are the bundles of vascular tubes which form the main veins. Then they begin to weaken also. It is not long before the weight of the leaf, the force of pelting rain, and late autumn's strong winds cause them to break and the leaf flutters to the ground.

Both those who collect leaves because of their beauty and those who study leaves because of their interest in science find autumn one of the most exciting seasons of the year. Leaves that are fascinating because of their color become even more fascinating if the collector understands the cause of color changes. Make the most of autumn days. Winter can come suddenly and with it autumn's carnival of color comes to an abrupt end.

herbals, herbariums, and leaf collections 6

Almost any region, uninteresting though it might seem at first glance, can be a fascinating area for the collector of leaves and plant specimens. So it was around Lund, a small village near the southern tip of Sweden, where Carolus Linnaeus (1707–1778) attended university in the early part of the eighteenth century. Young Linnaeus lived, as did most of the students who came to the University of Lund, in the home of one of the villagers. He was eager to learn about botany and it was his good fortune to have found lodging in the home of a physician who soon discovered the young man's interest in plants. The doctor lent him botany books from his library and showed him his collection of dried plant specimens, the first herbarium Linnaeus had seen. Immediately the young man began collecting material for an herbarium of his own, scouring the countryside, exploring the coastal areas, and gathering specimens to be dried, mounted on sheets of paper, and classified.

Linnaeus eventually became one of the world's great botanists. Botany, in his time, was a science dealing primarily with the identification and classification of plants. Scientists in many parts of Europe were accumulating specimens for herbariums— extensive collections that covered the flora of entire regions. In those days they were commonly called "dried gardens." By the time he was twenty-seven Linnaeus had an herbarium that included more than three thousand carefully dried and pressed specimens, each mounted on separate sheets and all of them from Sweden or Lapland. Years later he was asked to complete the classification of a large collection that had been gathered by an employee of the Dutch East India Company in Ceylon. This project gave him most of the information he needed for his book about the flora of Ceylon, published in 1748 while he was at the University of Uppsala. Poorly devised plant classifications had been used prior to Linnaeus's time. He developed one which is still used today, based largely upon the number of stamens and other parts of flowers; this was his greatest achievement.

Man's interest in leaves is an ancient one. In prehistoric times he searched for those which could be used for food or in constructing a shelter. He learned which were poisonous, often by bitter experience. Greek and Roman naturalists discovered many uses for leaves—such as the onions the Greeks obtained from Crete about 800 B.C., the cabbage grown in Greece in the third century or earlier—and how to prepare extracts from leaf tissues. It was not uncommon for an unscrupulous power-seeking individual to hire a professional poisoner who would use plant extracts to eliminate an adversary. In ancient times there were attempts at cataloging known plants, describing them, and giving their medicinal or practical use. What is believed to be the earliest treatise on the nature and classification of plants, *Historia Plantarum*, was written by Theophrastus (c. 380–287 B.C.), a naturalist of ancient Greece. The work earned him the epithet Father of Botanical Science.

Some of the early naturalists compiled herbals, which were treatises that described plants of some medicinal value. Plant classifications in ancient times consisted usually of three main categories—herbs, shrubs, and trees. The herbal became the principal source of botanical information in the latter part of the Middle Ages and the sixteenth century, when botany, as a true science, was nonexistent. An individual interested in this field usually attended university lectures in medicine. The invention of printing in western Europe from movable type about 1450 made possible large numbers of handsome books illustrated with woodcuts of the various species described in the text. Descriptions of medicinal uses of the plants were frequently worded to create a sort of mysticism about leaves, roots, and flowers from which concoctions could be made to soothe aches and irritations, allay fevers, reduce nausea, or cure some ailment. It was customary for medical students to make extensive studies of herbals in preparation for their profession.

Toward the end of the Middle Ages building an herbarium became a project that many found attractive. Luca Ghini (1500–1556), an Italian botanist, accumulated one of the first extensive collections of dried specimens of all kinds of plants. The idea spread from Italy to other countries of Europe. A stimulating factor was the discovery of the New World beyond the Atlantic and the opening of new trade routes to the Orient. Scientific journeys were undertaken to bring back specimens of the plants that grew in those regions. Botanists accompanied expeditions to the South Pacific, to the lands along the shores of the Indian Ocean, and to America. Then, in the seventeenth and eighteenth centuries, interest in leaves, roots, flowers, and in plants in general took a sudden spurt because those having medicinal value were finding ever-increasing use by doctors. The search was on for more species with curative powers, and ships carrying explorers and traders returned from distant lands with large quantities of plant specimens. Eventually interest extended to all kinds of plants, not merely those used in preparing remedies for aches and fevers. During the eighteenth century several large botanical gardens were established in some of Europe's major cultural centers. One of the more famous was the Royal Botanic Gardens at Kew, a suburb of London. It was founded in 1759. Today its herbarium has more than 6 million specimens, a vast reservoir of information for anyone wishing to identify unknown species or make surveys of the flora of a region in almost any part of the world.

Building an herbarium can be a fascinating hobby, but acquiring a leaf collection can be just as interesting and less difficult. The techniques required for each are much the same; however, a leaf collection requires no special equipment. The few materials needed can usually be found around the house. Making a collection of the leaves of plants native to the region in which you live will provide hours of interesting fun. Such a hobby can be worked into summer vacation plans and your leaf collection will then include specimens from other regions to which you might travel.

Botanists on a scientific expedition carry with them the same kinds of materials you will need—old newspapers and sheets of corrugated cardboard. Since they dry much greater numbers of leaves at a time, botanists may also bring along some relatively simple equipment such as a press made of lightweight frames

POPPY
LEAVES

Examples of
mounted leaf
specimens can
be seen on
pages 73–78.

BAMBOO
LEAVES

PALMATELY COMPOUND
LUPINE LEAVES

CHINESE MAPLE

AUTUMN LEAVES
OF THE PINK DOGWOOD

CEDAR

with felts and ventilators, a portable drier, and corrugated cardboard boxes for packing. For your purposes this added equipment is not really necessary. A century or two ago such expeditions were relatively rare and were usually spiced with adventure and hazards less common today. Thomas Johnson, a seventeenth-century English botanist, rode with several companions throughout most of England and Wales to collect specimens for a herbarium of the flora of those areas. It was the first expedition of its kind in Wales or any other region in Britain. Villagers were suspicious of their motives. In some places they encountered difficulties arising from such suspicions.

Keep in mind a few simple rules when you are building a leaf collection. Always collect specimens that are as nearly perfect as possible. Discard leaves with holes or tattered margins caused by the feasting of hungry insect larvae. Gather leaves that are average size for the species and carry them in a plastic bag to prevent excessive wilting before you have an opportunity to dry them. On your leaf-collecting excursions take along a small notebook so you can jot down the important characteristics of each kind of plant from which you have taken specimens, a brief description of the locality in which each was found, and accurate information about the location of the plant. Be sure to note the type of leaf arrangement. For small plants like herbs and grasses a good specimen of an entire plant should be taken.

Dry your leaf specimens as carefully and quickly as possible by placing them between sheets of newspaper. Many sheets with several leaves placed well apart on each sheet can be put between two large pieces of cardboard cut from cartons. Stack several of these layers atop one another in a warm dry place where they will not be disturbed and place a heavy object on top of the stack. Replace the damp sheets of newspaper with dry ones two or three times a week. If you dry leaf specimens quickly they will keep their natural color much better. It should take little more than a week to ten days to dry leaves of average size. A very satisfactory alternative for the collector with specimens that are not too large is to dry them between the pages of old catalogs, telephone directories, or magazines. Be sure, however, that they are not placed between the slick pages; use only the newsprint pages. They absorb moisture rapidly. Stack some books on top to create the pressure needed and move the specimens to another page every other day.

Care in mounting the dried specimens is as important as care in drying them. Lightweight show card or bristol board is excellent for mounts. It may be purchased from any dealer in art supplies. Standard herbarium sheets of the size used by most American botanists are made of heavy all-rag white paper 11½ by 16½ inches. European botanists use sheets that are longer. For a leaf collection smaller sheets, approximately 8½ by 12 inches, might prove satisfactory. Mount specimens of only one species on a sheet. A neat arrangement of several leaves on each mount, some showing the upper surface and others showing the undersurface, can be very attractive. A twig or stem flanked by two or three attached leaves might also prove artistic and scientifically useful. A leaf showing the characteristic autumn colors of the species can be included. Leave enough space in the lower right corner of the mount for the name of the species. Common names can be used, or, for the more ambitious collector, the scientific names can be traced and also included. Other data you might wish to include, such as the type of leaf, important leaf characteristics, the locality in which the specimen was found, your name, and the date, can be given on a label attached to the back of the mount.

Considerable originality can be shown in building a leaf collection if one is interested in art as well as in science. The artistically inclined collector will enjoy planning a creative arrangement of specimens and adding some lines of color to the mount to enhance the beauty of the leaves with an attractive background.

A strong, adhesivelike, fast-bonding Elmer's or LePage's glue and an effective procedure for applying it must be used. A floor tile or a square of window glass will make a good work surface. Spread the glue uniformly with a brush over a large area of the surface of the tile or glass. Then drop the dried specimen on the glue-coated area. After a few seconds lift it carefully, bring one end in contact with the mount, and lower the rest of it slowly until all of the specimen is in contact. There must be no wrinkles. Put a piece of waxed paper, then a piece of cardboard, on top, and press down on the mounted specimen. This step is to insure that all parts of the leaf's glue-coated surface will come in contact with the mount. Then remove the waxed paper and cardboard and set the mounted specimen aside for a couple of days to dry thoroughly.

There are several ways of providing the protection that the mounted leaves need. They can be kept in filing folders or stored in individual manila envelopes slightly larger than the mount. Another way is to cover each mounted specimen with a loose sheet of fairly heavy cellophane cut a little longer than the mount. The additional length will permit an edge at one end of the plastic sheet to be folded and glued to the back of the mount. Then the cellophane sheet will not only provide protection, but it can also be lifted up when the leaf must be examined more closely for such characteristics as texture and color. If the collection is not meant to meet rigid scientific requirements each specimen can be sprayed with a liquid plastic on both sides before it is mounted. This will, however, give some leaves an unnatural gloss and mask the natural texture. To the scientist, this would be removing a characteristic that might be important in plant identification.

A leaf collection can include photographs of leaves that are too large to dry or can be found only in parks, conservatories, or botanical gardens where you live. You can then include photographs of plants such as banana trees, palms, tree ferns, carnivorous plants, and many others. Some leaf collectors might prefer to restrict their activities to recording the many interesting leaves they find exclusively on photographic film. Prints from the negatives can then be mounted attractively in an album.

Since conservatories have a transparent dome or roofing to let in light, there is seldom any need to use a flash in taking photographs. It is always well, however, to use one or two stops (the size of the lens opening) larger than is recommended or a somewhat slower shutter speed. Since plant foliage is green and this is the color to which most black-and-white film is least sensitive, the larger stop or slower shutter speed will permit the longer exposure of the film that is needed. If leaf pictures are being made in a conservatory on color film and you are determining the correct exposure by using an exposure meter, take the reading for stop and shutter speed from a medium gray surface. For the subjects try to find leaves that are in uniform light, not spotty light made up of patches of bright sunlight mixed with areas of deep shadow. Select leaves that are more or less in the same plane so that fuzzy out-of-focus leaf images will not be a prominent part of the picture. Do not let poor results on your first few attempts discourage you. Many of the illustrations in this book were made from photographs taken by the author with a Rolleiflex camera on Eastman Tri-X film.

After Charles Darwin (1809–1882) published his *Origin of Species* in 1859, a natural basis for plant classification was adopted. Whether a plant belonged in a certain category was then determined by what fossil species scientists believed was its prehistoric ancestor or, in other words, upon its evolutionary development. Sometimes it is difficult to trace the origin of a species, so frequent changes have been made in modern systems of classification as discoveries are made regarding the kinship of certain living plants with those of early geological periods. As a consequence the number of divisions and subdivisions of the plant kingdom has been altered in recent years. One of the recent systems of classification has the entire kingdom divided into 24 divisions, among them the algae, fungus plants, ferns, liverworts, mosses, and seed-producers. Each division includes a number of classes and each class a number of smaller groups called orders which are subdivided into families. Each family usually includes several genera; each genus, a number of species.

A major contribution of Linnaeus to botanical science was the procedure he used in naming plants. He used Latin words in building the name of a plant—one for the genus to which it belongs followed by another for the species. This method is still used by botanists. Scientific research papers and reports have the names of plants in Latin instead of the common names by which they are known locally. A tree, shrub, or herb might be known by one common name in one region and an entirely different name in another. As a result, botanists find them creating too much confusion to be of any value in scientific work. A scientific name refers specifically to one kind of plant.

For example, the pineapple belongs to the genus *Ananus* and the species *comosus*. Its scientific name is *Ananus comosus*. The sugar maple is a member of the genus *Acer*, as are all of the other kinds of maples. But it also belongs to the species *saccharum*. If you have mounted leaf specimens of this tree in your collection, the label in the lower right corner of the mount, if both common and scientific names were given, would read sugar maple (*Acer saccharum* Marsh.). The "Marsh." is an abbreviation to indicate who first gave the plant its name. The red maple is *A. rubrum* L. The abbreviation L. is for Linnaeus. The scientific names of other maples include the silver maple, *A. saccharinum* Marsh.;

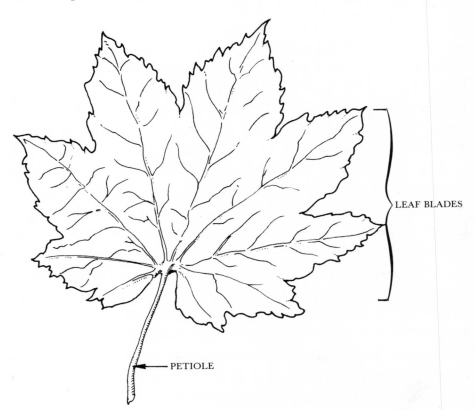

LEAF BLADES

PETIOLE

Drawing showing the pattern of the veins and the major parts of a maple leaf. It is palmately netted-veined.

vine maple, *A. circinatum* Pursch; and mountain maple, *A. spicatum* Lamb.

Leaf collectors look to the vascular plants, those with a system of tubes for conducting fluids, as the most rewarding source of leaf specimens. They need not focus their attention on other divisions since the divisions included among the vascular plants have the true leaves. The scientific names of the large groups vary with the system of classification used. One modern system groups them in two divisions—the Pteridophyta (ferns) and Spermatophyta (seed-producers), the latter divided still further into the Gymnospermae (cone-bearers) and the Angiospermae (flowering plants).

An ambitious collector, baffled in his efforts to learn the name of a plant from which he has taken leaves, should take note of as many characteristics of the plant as possible at the time the leaves are collected. Any good library will have the manuals or keys to the flora of different regions, so that you can trace both the scientific and common names through the characteristics of a plant. Manuals have been published for most of the states as well as the provinces of Canada. Look for the key for the region in which you collected a specimen and browse through it to learn how to use it properly. Then choose a couple of plants you know well and use their major characteristics to trace through the key to their scientific and common names.

Once you become familiar with a manual, discovering the names of plants represented by specimens in your leaf collection will prove to be more fun than working crossword puzzles. Do not hesitate to collect specimens from plants you are unable to identify at the moment in the field. The names can be traced from leaf characteristics and notes you have kept about the plant months or years after they have been dried and mounted.

leaves of the
7 flowering plants

The flowering plants make up the group botanists call the *angiosperms,* the highest division of the plant kingdom. Trees, shrubs, and herbs that develop flowers to produce seeds are included in this large group. In angiosperms the seeds form in the ovary of the flower rather than being exposed directly to the air. As the seeds develop the ovary wall becomes a protective covering.

Angiosperms dominate the plant life of our planet. Each type of environment provides conditions favorable to the growth of many kinds of angiosperms ranging from small herbs to shrubs in cold regions and to trees in regions where the temperature range creates a mild climate. Some prefer a shallow water environment. Water lilies with oval leaves floating on the surface of the margins of lakes or sloughs are striking examples of this type of angiosperm. Others thrive best in swamps. In

sharp contrast to aquatic or semiaquatic species are the
angiosperms of the desert country with leaf modifications that
enable them to conserve their meager supply of water and
protect them from the heat of intense sunlight. The grasses and
small flowering plants of the plains and the prairies: shade-
loving violets, trilliums, and tiger lilies, shrubs like the wild rose
and its close relative, the wild strawberry, are all angiosperms
fitted to live in a specific type of surroundings. When the long
days of summer arrive for a brief spell in the Far North small
flowering plants bring patches of color to its usually drab
wastelands. Although most of the angiosperms are deciduous,
some, such as the laurels, the madrona, and the rhododendrons,
are evergreen and able to grow where winter temperatures are

The oval leaves of the
water lily are adapted by
nature to function
perfectly in a water
environment.

not extremely low and moisture is plentiful. Those angiosperms which are trees often have flowers that are quite inconspicuous because of their greenish-yellow color. The grasses have flower clusters so small they often pass unnoticed. So great is the number of species of angiosperms and so widely are they distributed that collecting leaf specimens of just part of the many thousands of kinds would require years and years of exploring. To do a more thorough job restrict your leaf-collecting to representatives that live in a specific type of habitat or are native to a certain geographical area. Interesting leaf collections can be made of specimens of plants that are included in one or two closely related families.

Botanists use seed and leaf characteristics to distinguish between the two large groups of angiosperms, the *monocotyledons* and *dicotyledons* (more commonly called *monocots* and *dicots*). The seeds of the monocots, as the name implies, have but one cotyledon. These are the seed leaves of the embryo plant which are modified to store food in concentrated form for use when the seed sprouts and the young plant begins to develop. They keep the young plant alive and growing until true leaves with green chlorophyll take over the task. Lilies, tulips, hyacinths, cereal grains, orchids, the banana plant, and the pineapple are just a few examples of the many thousands of species of monocots. Dicots have two such seed leaves. Lima beans, a familiar dicot, planted in a garden or a flowerpot, show their prominent cotyledons when they sprout and push them above the soil. They are kidney-shaped and either white or very pale green. As their stored food is used by the young plant they become less conspicuous, shrivel, and eventually drop to the ground.

The leaf characteristic that distinguishes between the monocots and dicots is venation. The leaves of the monocots have

The leaves of the banana tree have parallel venation. In most leaves with parallel venation the veins run from the base to the tip of the blade parallel to the midrib. Banana leaves have the veins parallel across the leaf blade, perpendicular to the midrib.

their principal veins parallel or nearly parallel. In the dicots the leaves are either palmately or pinnately netted-veined. A net of small veins, some so small they can be seen only with the aid of a microscope, link the major veins of each pattern. The leaves of corn, the grasses, and cereal plants such as wheat, rice, oats, and rye are parallel-veined, the major veins extending from the tip to the base. Others, like the banana, have parallel veins extending across the leaf blade from midrib to margin.

Since venation is so important a characteristic in distinguishing monocots from dicots, an interesting addition to a leaf collection would be a few specimens with all of the green tissue removed. These would show the arrangement of the veins very clearly. Each will be a delicate lacelike specimen. These are often called *leaf skeletons*. They are more easily prepared from the leaves of some species than others. Leaves with a very tough surface layer are not recommended and neither are those so thin and fragile they can easily be torn. A safe and simple way to remove the green tissues is to let nature do the work. Careful handling of the leaves and considerable patience is all that is needed to be successful in this method. Select the most perfect specimens for skeletonizing. It is well to prepare several of each kind of venation pattern. Put them in a large glass jar and fill to within a few inches of the top with water. Leave it in a warm dark place in a storeroom, basement, or other place where it can stand through the winter without being disturbed but can still be checked conveniently. Within a few days millions of microscopic plants and animals will be feeding upon the soft leaf tissues. Since this is a process or form of rotting, gases with objectionable odors will rise from the mixture, so choose a place for the jar which is more or less isolated. Do not let the water level in the jar drop so far as to expose some of the leaves to the air above the liquid or they will dry, warp, and curl. Add tap water occasionally to prevent this from happening.

The second step in the skeletonizing will be carried out in the spring. Carefully remove a specimen from the mixture and put it on a piece of tile or window glass. With a brush such as is used in painting with watercolors, gently remove the decayed tissue

LEAF SKELETONS

from both surfaces of the leaf. Do not use a stiff brush. Also do not use much pressure. After brushing lift the specimen carefully and rinse in a pan of water to remove loose particles still clinging to it. Then put it between two pieces of blotting paper until most of the moisture has been absorbed. Complete the drying in the same way that other leaf specimens are dried. After a few days the leaf skeleton can be mounted on a black mount in the usual way.

Leaf collectors must keep in mind that there are restrictions on collecting leaves, flowers, and plants in certain areas. Any who ignore these restrictions can be subject to fines or other penalties. Despite this there are always plenty of places where an abundance of specimens can be obtained to meet the needs of even the most enthusiastic leaf-collectors. Collecting of plant material is normally prohibited in city parks and playgrounds, in the grounds around public buildings, and in state and national historic sites and parks. Many states make an effort to protect the wild flowers within their borders by prohibiting picking them. Never collect plant material from private property without first asking the permission of the owners. In most cases permission will be granted if the reason for desiring such material is explained. If permission is given never abuse the privilege by taking more than is needed or carelessly damaging plants from which specimens are taken.

It is surprising what a variety of leaves can be gathered from the plants in your own backyard. A flower garden or a plot where vegetables are grown is also a source of excellent material. Potted plants, a window box, a weed patch, a vacant lot, and country roadsides will provide more. Most fortunate are the leaf-hunters who live near forests, marshes, woodlands bordering a river, or trails that lead into mountain or desert regions.

The families of the angiosperms are extremely interesting. Species you probably would not consider related are often found in the same family. Frequently, neither the common nor the scientific name of a plant gives a clue to the family to which it belongs, so you will need to refer to some good reference book about plant classification or taxonomy, a manual or guide to the flora of the region in which you live, and perhaps an encyclopedia for the information needed. Select an angiosperm family that interests you and is well represented among the plants that can be found in your locality. Then begin collecting specimens of the leaves of as many as can be found.

A family of angiosperms well represented in the temperate regions of North America is the pea family. Scientists speak of them as *legumes*. Some of its members are not native to this continent, but they now grow abundantly across the United States and Canada. Many of them were brought here by pioneer farmers who came from Europe. All have compound leaves. Their flowers are constructed like those of the well-known sweet pea. Legumes usually have their seeds enclosed in a pod. Various species can be found in farming country, meadowlands, and on the prairies. The family also includes the many species of clover, vetch, and alfalfa that are grown by farmers as fodder for cattle. The kinds of Scotch broom and lupine growing in poor soil along roadsides and on cliffs that overlook the sea are legumes. Locoweed and wild licorice common in some areas on the plains are also members of this group.

One of the largest families of angiosperms in the order Liliales is the Liliaceae, with more than 2,500 species. The Liliaceae has many members native to North America. Their leaves are parallel-veined and spring from a bulb usually in the form of a rosette at the base of the stem. All of us are quite familiar with some of the wild and cultivated species. Among them are the lily of the valley, tulip, hyacinth, Easter lily, daffodil, and trillium that brighten our flower gardens or flourish in shady spots along woodland trails. One interesting group in the family consists of shrubs and trees that are plentiful in desert areas of the Southwest and in the sandy regions of

The aloe, a succulent which grows abundantly in South Africa, has a rosette of thick fleshy triangular leaves for storing food and fluids and clusters of narrow leaves atop the tall flower stems that rise from the rosette.

some southeastern states—the yuccas. A typical example is the Spanish bayonet with thick stiff leaves having sharp knifelike margins and a tip like that of a spear. Few desert animals dare attempt to feed upon this spiny plant or rob it of the fruit that develops after its huge clusters of creamy-white blossoms wither. One of the more spectacular members of this order of the lily family is the Joshua tree. It grows to heights of 35 feet or more, with branches shooting out from the main trunk at awkward angles. It develops large clusters of bell-shaped white flowers in March or April. These beautiful trees can be seen in the half-million-acre Joshua Tree National Monument in southern California east of Los Angeles and along the Joshua Forest Parkway in Arizona northwest of Wickenburg. A leaf collector would find it impractical to add leaf specimens of the Joshua tree to his collection because of their size and protective armor, and the great difficulty in drying them. These provide, therefore, a splendid example of leaves which should be photographed. Attractive photographs can be made of many species of yucca on a vacation trip in Arizona, New Mexico, or southern California.

It is quite a surprise to most leaf hunters that water lilies are not included in the lily family. The water lily family, known to the botanist as the Nymphaeaceae, consists of dicots, instead of monocots as in the lily family. Their floating blossoms and leaves are attached to long, tough stems rooted in the mud of lake beds, slowly moving streams, or stagnant ponds. In some species the stems that support the blossoms extend above the surface of the water. The leaves are more or less circular, with a single deep notch where they join the stem. The most interesting member of the family is the royal water lily *(Victoria amazonica)*, a native of the jungle regions of the Amazon Valley. It has huge

Leaves of the Joshua trees
of Arizona and southern
California are modified
for protection by having
sharp cutting edges and
spear-point tips.

Large floating leaves several feet in diameter are characteristic of *Victoria amazonica*, the royal water lily.

oval leaves several feet in diameter which float on the surface of the water. Each leaf has an upturned edge extending three or four inches above the water and on the underside a network of large veins radiating from the center. The royal water lily was brought to England nearly 150 years ago, and the first attempts to grow the plant were unsuccessful. But the scientists and gardeners at The Royal Botanic Gardens at Kew were persistent, and eventually, in the 1840s, their efforts were rewarded. *Victoria amazonica* is now a great attraction in the major botanical gardens of Europe and the United States. The blossoming period, when the showy fragrant flowers open each night for a week or more, is an event which draws many visitors. Photographs of water lily leaves will enhance any leaf collection.

The pineapple family of monocots is another family with many interesting species. Most of us must rely on botanical gardens to enjoy them unless we are fortunate enough to visit the pineapple fields in Hawaii. The pineapple plant has a rosette of thick leaves which spring from the base of its very short central stem. The parts of its blossoms are clustered and fused together to create the large fruit that in some ways resembles a huge pine cone in shape. Atop the pineapple is another cluster of short leaves.

The underside of a royal water lily (*Victoria amazonica*) leaf.

A plant many of us might consider out of place in this group is the Florida moss, also known quite commonly as Spanish moss. It drapes in long streamers over the branches of live oaks and cypress trees throughout the South. Each streamer consists of lengthy gray-green stems difficult to distinguish from the stemlike leaves of the same color. The common name is very misleading because the plant is not in fact a moss, but a monocot belonging to the pineapple family.

The pineapple *(Ananas)* plant has thick stiff leaves growing as a rosette on a short thick stem. At the top of the stem a conelike fruit is formed by the fusing together of the individual flowers of a large flower cluster. A second rosette of leaves forms at the top of the pineapple.

Leaf hunters who live in Florida, the Carolinas, and some neighboring states are familiar with a number of kinds of carnivorous plants. Those who do not live in this region can find them in botanical gardens or purchase them at low cost in stores where potted houseplants are sold. The leaves of these plants are so modified that they are difficult to dry and mount, but they are easily photographed. In most cases the leaves are highly specialized for trapping and digesting insects. The Venus flytrap is an expert in this respect. Its leaves grow from the base of the plant in a rosette arrangement. Some lie flat on the ground for most of their length; others stand erect from the central part of the rosette. Much of the leaf blade is a long spatula-shaped structure that is flat and very narrow. Near its tip this flattened part terminates and the blade widens from the midrib to form two flat halves hinged together along the central main vein. These form the trap, a modified section of the blade with tough flexible hairs along the margins. Additional sharp toothlike structures are on the inner surface of each of the two flaps. When a fly or a gnat comes in contact with the marginal hairs it triggers the flaps to snap together and crush the insect. The marginal hairs hold the trap shut while glands in the leaf tissue secrete a digestive juice which engulfs the victim. For about one dollar a Venus flytrap can be purchased at a variety store like Woolworth's. It will come in a packet with moss and instructions for planting it and giving it the proper care. Let it occupy a sunny indoor window ledge and by the time its pale green leaves are fully developed watch the drama of a carnivorous plant capturing its insect prey.

Both the sundew and the Venus flytrap are members of the sundew family. But the sundew captures its prey in a somewhat different way than its close relative. Sticky leaves, each a

Many species of
carnivorous plants belong
to the sundew family.
Their leaves are modified
for trapping insects.
Drosera capensis, shown
here, has leaf hairs that
secrete a sticky fluid.

circular pad, are at the tips of stems that radiate from the center
of the base of the plant. Each is covered with hairy tentacles. A
fly that alights on one of these quickly finds some of the
tentacles folding over it while it becomes more entangled in the
sticky secretion that coats the pad. Escape is practically
impossible. Then the process of digesting the prey begins.

The pitcher plant, another of the carnivorous group, uses a
different way to catch insects. Its modified leaves form a pitcher

rimmed at its lip with teeth, topped by a flap or lid some color other than green, and exuding a foul odor. There are several varieties of this plant in most tropical regions. Sharp bristles slant downward from the inner surface of the pitcher. The foul smell that attracts insects to the plant comes from the liquid inside the pitcher in which trapped insects are being digested or have been decomposed. Insects have no difficulty making their way into the pitcher, but the sticky fluids coating the inner surface of its walls and the sharp bristles slanting downward make it impossible for them to find their way out. The victims eventually drop into the fluid, are digested, and the digested food, largely amino acid, is absorbed by the plant.

But an excellent leaf collection can also be built with less exotic and unusual species of angiosperms. Thousands of species grouped in families with hundreds of species in each family can be readily discovered in meadows, woodlands, grasslands, and forests in the region where you live.

There are many families of trees among the angiosperms that will provide excellent specimens of leaves for your collection. One of the largest is the willow family, which is well represented in the temperate regions of the United States and Canada. It includes not only the true willow group, but also a group known as poplars, which is made up of poplars, aspens, and cotton-woods. All are trees that grow very rapidly and become deeply rooted in the soil.

In the willow family, Salicaceae, lance-shaped leaves arranged alternately on the twigs are characteristic of the members of the principal genus, *Salix*. Some species of this genus thrive best in moist soil along river banks and throughout lush valleys. The black willow, *Salix nigra* Marsh., a species widely distributed in the eastern United States, has smooth-surfaced

One of the species of the pussy willow tree known scientifically as *Salix discolor*.

leaves that are dark green on both sides and up to six inches in length, and have finely toothed or serrated margins. The weeping willow, *S. babylonica* L., originally a native of China, was brought to America many years ago. It has leaves similar to the black willow, but dark green on the upper surface and silvery gray-green underneath. The pussy willow, *S. discolor* Muhl., is more of a shrub than a tree and has lance-shaped leaves that are somewhat oblong and seldom over four inches long. The leaves of the shining willow, *S. lucida* Muhl., are distinctive in being shiny on both sides. If you explore the woodlands and valleys of the region in which you live you undoubtedly will find other species of genus *Salix*, and by noting their leaf characteristics you will be able to trace their scientific and common names.

Consult a tree manual to learn what species of the genus *Populus*, commonly called poplars, you might expect to find. Some species in this genus of the willow family bear common names other than poplar, such as aspen and cottonwood. Perhaps you will find the quaking aspen, *Populus tremuloides* Michx. This species is very numerous on mountain ranges in areas where, years earlier, fires have wiped out large areas of forest. The tree gets its name because its leaves, attached to twigs by a leaf stem or petiole that is flattened, quiver and dance in the slightest breeze. The leaves, unlike those of other species in this big family, have a circular blade. The margin of each is serrated, the notches forming slightly rounded teeth. Balsam poplar, *P. tacamahaca* Mill., has ovate leaves with an upper surface that is smooth and an undersurface that in some specimens might bear rust-colored spots. A species which was introduced from Europe is known by the common name, white poplar. A little exploring might lead to good leaf specimens of the swamp cottonwood, *P. heterophylla* L.; eastern cottonwood, *P. deltoides* Marsh.; and several other species belonging to this genus.

The beech family is another large family of deciduous trees. It includes a large variety of species such as the American beech, American chestnut, and a long list of oaks with considerable variation in leaf shapes. The olive family, represented in the temperate zones of the United States only by a number of species of ash, is another very interesting group.

Flower gardens, orchards, and berry patches should be explored. The rose family offers a great variety of species, both wild and cultivated. In addition to roses it includes among its members the meadowsweet, spiraeas, and plants of some commercial value such as the strawberry, peach, quince, cherry, raspberry, and a number of other shrubs and fruit trees. An equally interesting group is the mustard family with a great number of species that are commonly called weeds. Others in the mustard family help contribute to the attractiveness of many a flower garden. There are also some species included that are common vegetable plants like the radish, turnip, cabbage, and cauliflower. These and other angiosperms can provide ample material for the most enthusiastic leaf collector.

leaves of the
8 cone-bearers

Nature designed the leaves of the cone-bearers to withstand the rigors of a hostile environment. The trees of this large category of plants mantle the headlands along much of the seacoast of America where winter storms bring driving sleet and snow. At high altitudes they grow to the borders of the barren wastes along the backbone of mountain ranges and a few stunted species eke out an existence in desert country. Although vast forests of cone-bearers spread across river basins, mountains, and the hills and valleys of our coastal regions, nature has constructed them to bend under the force of gales, to thrive in poor soil, and to withstand exposure to long periods of subzero temperatures. A broadleaf tree such as a maple or chestnut could not survive under the conditions to which cone-bearers are sometimes exposed.

The cone-bearers, also known as conifers, range in size from small inconspicuous plants to the world's tallest trees—the sequoias and the Douglas firs. Some species have cones the size of thimbles, while others have cones nearly two feet long. Their seeds cling to the scales of the cones. Some seeds are equipped with winglike appendages which help to carry them considerable distances from the parent tree when they are ripe and ready to fall to the forest floor. Unlike the seeds of the angiosperms, conifer seeds are naked; they are not protected by an ovary wall. Botanists class these plants as *gymnosperms.*

The species of gymnosperms are much easier to identify than the species of other groups in the plant kingdom. The major leaf characteristics that are helpful in identification are the color (green, yellowish or bluish green), the average length, the usual arrangement on twigs, the number of needles in a bundle, and the shape. The color and texture of the bark, the size and shape of cones, and the height and shape of the tree supplement leaf characteristics in identification. If you make notes of these clues, identification will be easy.

The leaves of the cone-bearers are true leaves with veins and resin ducts built of the cells of the vascular tissue. Nature patterned them to withstand severe cold and periods of drought. Their thick epidermis is covered by a heavy cuticle, or waxy coating. Unlike the angiosperms with their broad leaf blades and numerous stomata, the needles are narrow and stomata are distributed very sparsely over the surface. Needles are arranged in a variety of ways on twigs and branches, each species having a definite characteristic pattern.

Most of the conifers with leaves that are needles are not deciduous. A well-known exception, however, is the larch. Its needles turn yellow in late autumn and by the time winter storms have spread a mantle of snow across the forest floor they have fallen from its branches.

There are many kinds of conifers that have scalelike leaves instead of needles. The individual scales are small and usually overlap on the branchlets in a pattern of whorls which is characteristic of the species to which the tree belongs. These scales seldom attain a length greater than one-quarter of an inch; in most species they are one-eighth to one-quarter inch long. The trees commonly called cedars have scalelike leaves which contain aromatic oils that give off, in certain species, a pleasant odor.

Pine needles withstand the rigors of summer heat and severe winter cold. In most species the needles are in clusters of two, three, four, or five, each cluster attached to a branch or twig. The number of needles per cluster is a characteristic of the species to which the tree belongs. Unlike the leaves of deciduous trees, the needles of a conifer remain attached and serve the tree for several years.

The pine family includes most of the cone-bearers. An interesting group within this family is made up of several species of nut pines or piñons. One of these is *Pinus edulis*, the scrubby gnarled piñon of the mesa country in the American Southwest. Its needles, about one-and-a-half inches in length and dark green, are usually in bunches of two on its branches. The

Conifers thrive in relatively poor soil and can endure marked seasonal changes in temperature and in water supply. Typical of the areas favorable to the growth of conifers is the region that includes the mountain slopes in and around Lassen Volcanic National Park in northern California.

scientific name was derived from the fact that the large seeds or nuts produced on its cones are an important food harvested by the Apaches, Comanches, Navajos, and other Indians of the Southwest. *Edulis* means edible. The big seeds of the single-leaf piñon are also an important food of the Indians, particularly in Nevada. This is a species of nut pine quite widely distributed throughout the mountain and desert country of the Great Basin which reaches from southern Idaho to Nevada, southern California, and parts of western Arizona. It differs from other pines in having needles that occur singly on its twigs and branches. The scientific name is *Pinus monophylla* which means single leaf.

Several species of pine are important as sources of lumber. The eastern white pine with a straight trunk reaching around 200 feet into the sky was in great demand during the colonial period and well into the nineteenth century when ships were sailing to Europe and new lands were being explored along the rim of the Pacific. The trees were cut in the forests along the northeastern coast and westward into Pennsylvania and the Great Lakes region. Then the branches were trimmed from the trunk, the bark peeled away, and the trunks taken to the New England shipbuilding yards to be used as masts. The eastern white pine, like the western white pine which grows in Rocky Mountain and Pacific Coast forests, has its needles in bundles of five. Other pines found in the West that have their needles in bundles of five include the sugar pine of the mountains skirting the Pacific Coast, the hickory pine, and the limber pine. The loblolly pine is one of the most valuable sources of timber. It is found in the southern states and up the east coast from northern Florida to southern New Jersey. Its trunk is seldom as large as the trunks of the white pines which frequently have a diameter of six feet. Loblolly pine needles sometimes reach lengths of almost a foot and are pale green in color.

The hemlock, spruce, and fir of the pine family are other cone-bearers which are valuable sources of timber. The leaves of all three are needles. Both the hemlocks and firs have two rows of needles, one row opposite the other on either side of each branchlet. All three of these conifers are commonly in demand for use as Christmas trees during the holiday season. These are the young trees that are thinned out of the forests to eliminate overcrowding or are grown on tree farms.

A tree with no value for lumber because of its slender trunk is the lodgepole pine. It forms immense dark forests in the wide trenches made during past geological periods by huge glaciers that bulldozed their way across the ranges of the Rockies and the mountains of northern British Columbia. Forests of lodgepole pine cover thousands of square miles. These trees get their name from the use that was made of them by the Indians. Several tribes found them ideal for the supporting structure of their tepees or lodges. They were long and strong enough to hold up the weight of the covering of animal skins of which the lodge was made. The bright yellowish-green needles of the lodgepole pine are, on the average, about three inches long. They are in clusters or bundles with two needles in each bundle.

A number of species of cone-bearers which are commonly called cedars are incorrectly named, according to botanists. They rely on scientific names in identifying plants. From the scientific viewpoint the name *cedar* should be applied only to those species in the genus *Cedrus*. The cedar of Lebanon, the deodar tree of India, and an alpine African tree called the Atlas cedar meet this requirement. None of these three are native to North America. There are a number of species having *cedar* as part of their common name but none of these belong to the genus *Cedrus*. These are species botanists call "false cedars."

Among the "cedars" some species belong to the genus *Thuja*. The western red cedar and the northern white cedar are examples. The leaves of the former are tiny green scales that cling closely to the branchlets; those of the latter are even smaller—usually no longer than an eighth of an inch. Western red cedar grows along the Pacific Coast where there is an abundance of rain. Its range extends all the way from Alaska to northern California. Today it is one of America's major sources of timber for lumber and shingles. Indians used to strip the tough fibrous bark from the trunk for making ropes and weaving baskets and mats. Northern white cedar is native to the forests around the Great Lakes and is abundant in Canada from the shores of the Atlantic in the Maritime Provinces as far westward as the southern part of Manitoba. Port Orford cedar, a species belonging to the genus *Champaecyparis*, is very restricted in its distribution. It is native to a region that skirts the Pacific Ocean from southern Oregon to northern California, where rainfall is heavy in autumn, winter, and early spring. Its leaves are seldom more than half the length of the scales of the western red cedar. Its wood gives off a distinctive and pleasant odor.

The canoe cedar, like other species of false cedars, belongs to the cypress family of the conifers. Its branchlets are also covered with overlapping leaf scales. The Indians who lived in the Pacific Northwest before the coming of the white man relied upon the canoe cedar to provide many of the materials to meet their needs. Tribal chiefs and other very important members of a tribe sometimes held a potlatch with gift-giving, feasting, speeches, and other festivities to impress their friends and neighbors. Invariably for the great event one of the finest canoe cedars that could be found in the forest near the village was selected for a totem pole. A totem-carver was chosen to use his skill in carving the raven, fish, bear, beaver, and other animals that might symbolize important happenings in the life of the man for whom the pole was being prepared. Eventually, after many weeks of work, it was erected in a conspicuous place near his lodge in the village where the potlatch was to be held. Some tribes, particularly the Haidas who lived along the coast of British Columbia, carved their war canoes from these cedars. Their womenfolk were skilled in weaving baskets, blankets, and ropes from the fibers of the bark stripped from the trees.

Collectors who include the gymnosperms in their leaf collection will want a small branchlet of the Douglas fir. The needles are distinctive enough to serve as a major clue in identifying this species which has become the principal source of lumber in the United States. They are dark green tinged with either yellow or blue and normally vary in length from slightly more than half an inch to one and a quarter inches. The pointed tip of each needle, a distinct groove on the upper surface of the leaf blade, and a white band flanking either side of the midrib on the undersurface provide a combination of leaf characteristics that definitely identify the tree. The Douglas fir is one of the giants of American forests. The huge trunk measures well over eight or nine feet in diameter near the base and often reaches skyward more than three hundred feet in many specimens, heights surpassed only by members of the redwood family. Botanists have difficulty in agreeing on how the Douglas fir should be classified. Some claim it is a "false" hemlock. Others recognize some of its characteristics as being those of the yew.

The true giants of the cone-bearers belong to the redwood family and the genus *Sequoia*. They are the California redwood

This is one of the trees of
the Monterey cypress
which grows along the
shore of Carmel Bay in
California. Its twigs are
covered with dark green
scalelike leaves like other
members of the cypress
family.

The Douglas fir is one of
the most widely
distributed conifers in
North America. This one
is rooted among the rocks
and poor soil at high
altitudes along the rim of
Crater Lake in Oregon.

and the giant sequoias, or big trees, as they are commonly called. The redwoods are usually the taller of the two; however, the big trees have enormous trunks that make them more impressive. Redwoods grow along a strip of the Pacific Coast from the state border in southeastern Oregon to Santa Cruz, about 50 miles south of San Francisco. The big trees thrive in a relatively small area on the western side of the Sierra Nevada Mountains in California. They are the ancient members of the redwood family. The age of many specimens has been determined to be between three and four thousand years, whereas redwoods are seldom found that are much older than two thousand years. The big trees prefer to grow at altitudes around 4,500 feet. The redwoods thrive along the coast where heavy fog rolls inland at least a part of almost every day. Both must have an abundance of moisture. Both species have scale-type dark green leaves. In the big trees these scales average a little more than an eighth of an inch in length; in the redwoods they are somewhat longer.

Much of the vast redwood forest that covered the coastal regions in the last century is gone today because of the demand for lumber. Some years ago a league was formed to work for the protection of the giant trees that still remained. In 1968 one of the league's goals was partly attained when a series of large groves of giant redwoods along the northern California coast was set aside as the Redwood National Park.

The species of cone-bearers that have been mentioned are merely a sampling of some of the hundreds of species native to North America. Specimens of needles or needle clusters can be easily obtained from many of the good representative kinds. Areas in forests where logging operations are in progress or land is being cleared are excellent for obtaining fine specimens.

Mounting dried specimens on cardboard is not a satisfactory method for displaying branchlets of cone-bearers that have needles for leaves. When the needles are thoroughly dry they will easily drop from the specimen even with the most careful handling. Containers called Riker mounts can be used instead. These are shallow boxes with a glass top. A neatly cut sheet of absorbent cotton that fits the box serves as a cushion for the specimen. But Riker mounts are relatively expensive. Both the novice and the experienced collector can provide similar mounts if they use boxes with neatly fitting transparent plastic covers of the type used in packaging notepaper, cards, and other items obtained in stationery stores or from dealers in office supplies. Save these containers for specimens you might wish to mount and purchase a roll of absorbent cotton from which you can cut the cushion to place under them.

Specimens of cone-bearers with scalelike leaves can be mounted in the same way that dried leaves of the angiosperms and ferns are mounted. Select only one or two of the smallest branchlets from a cedar, cypress, or redwood and press them between newspapers under considerable weight. Then mount them in the usual way.

9 the ferns

An observant leaf hunter who can explore the woodlands and forests of a large region is fortunate indeed. He will surely venture from well-known trails into shady recesses where, even on a summer day, it is cool and damp. The earth is matted with fallen leaves and patches of moss cling to boulders and tree trunks. Beside a rotting log he will probably find a clump of ferns rising above the anemones and trilliums which are also shade-loving plants.

Ferns are today's representatives of an ancient flora that flourished in the warm humid environment of an era when giant reptiles dominated the earth. Many species grow in most of the temperate regions of the world, but the rain forests of tropical regions have the greatest variety of this type of plant life. Across America there are species that are very different in their liking for shade or sunlight, swamplands or cliffside rock ledges, rich humus or sandy soil. There are marsh ferns, handsome cinnamon ferns that love the dampness of the swamp, and sensitive ferns that thrive along lake shores. The Christmas fern remains green when snow blankets the rocky wooded areas which are its favorite haunt. The hart's-tongue has long leathery leaves so different from the leaves of most ferns it is often mistaken for a member of some other family of plants. In the coastal forests of the Pacific Northwest and in the Everglades of Florida some species live on the moss-covered branches and trunks of trees. They are *epiphytes*—nonparasitic plants that do not take food from the tree on which they grow, but obtain the materials needed to sustain life from the air, decaying moss, and the moisture that trickles down the tree's branches and trunk.

The leaves of ferns are called *fronds*. They are true leaves like those of the oak and maple with veins and a network of conducting cells that are part of their vascular system. Some are light green in color. Other species, in which the mesophyll tissue is heavily laden with chlorophyll, have dark green fronds. The stomata are on the underside of the leaflets to permit carbon dioxide to reach the mesophyll and oxygen to escape during photosynthesis, and also to permit the movement of these gases in the opposite direction during respiration.

Fern fronds are the most important part of the plant. They function not only as leaves usually function, but also produce the spores that are involved in reproduction. In the majority of species the spores are formed on the underside of the frond, enclosed in small sacs which are known as *sporangia*. The sporangia are usually clustered together to form a *sorus*, although they may also occur singly. If you examine a frond of the common sword fern look for brown or black dots on the underside arranged in a definite pattern along the veins. There are also species of ferns in which the sori are found along the margin of each leaflet. In this case the edge of the leaflet curves down and inward to provide protection for the spores. There are a few species producing their sporangia at the tip of their fronds which are modified to form stalks. The characteristic way in

The sago palm is a cycad with leaves similar to those of many ferns. It is classed in the same group as ferns, but it reproduces by seeds instead of spores. It is found in the United States in the Florida Keys. The leaves are pinnately compound.

The fronds of the sword fern so common in the forests of the Pacific Northwest are long, tapering, and divided into many leaflets. Brown spore cases appear on their undersurface in late summer.

which the sporangia are distributed on the fronds, their shape, and their color are major clues used in identifying the various species.

Several kinds of ferns supplement their role as spore-producers with another way of creating new plants. The walking fern is an excellent example. The fronds of this species are unusually long and are not divided into leaflets or *pinnae*. The base of the blade is heart-shaped. When the tip of the tonguelike portion touches the ground it develops roots and a new plant begins to grow. Eventually the leaf tip dries up and the young plant separates from the parent plant. This is a method quite like the propagation of strawberry plants by means of runners. The few long stems that grow from the strawberry plant are the runners. As they grow in length they bend downward and eventually touch the ground. Roots develop from the stem where it touches the soil and directly above them the upper part of a new plant makes its appearance. In the walking fern, however, it is a leaf tip and not a stem which produces the new plant.

The stems of most of the different species of ferns are underground and extend horizontally in the soil. Botanists call these stems *rhizomes*. When conditions become favorable in the spring roots grow downward from the rhizomes to penetrate deep into the soil and from their upper surface leaf stalks eventually grow and push above the soil. The usual purpose of a stem is to support the leaves and to conduct water and other fluids. The rhizomes have an additional function. They store food, largely in the form of starch, to contribute to the rapid growth of the young ferns which are developing. Since most ferns are perennials, which is to say they live from year to year, there must be some additional food provided for the new shoots until they can manufacture enough to meet their requirements.

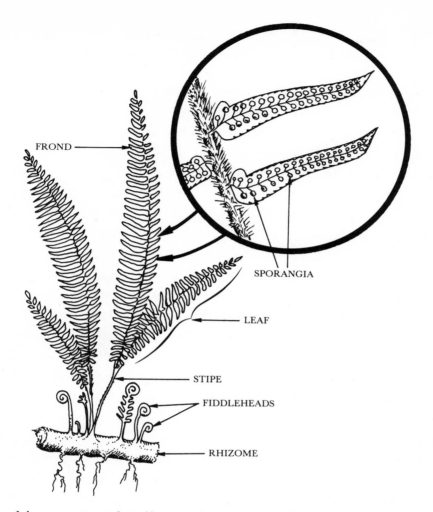

FROND

SPORANGIA

LEAF

STIPE

FIDDLEHEADS

RHIZOME

Parts of the sword fern and a section of the underside of several leaflets of a frond showing the position of the sporangia.

The rhizomes remain alive underground throughout the winter months. The fronds do not survive beyond the first few frosts of late autumn except in those varieties that are evergreen ferns. The excess sugars produced in the green tissues of the fronds during the warm days of summer when photosynthetic activity is at its peak are dissolved in plant fluids, conducted to the rhizomes, and converted to starch to be stored.

The first shoots that come through the soil in the spring usually have the knoblike fiddlehead at their tip. This is actually a leaf bud formed of a tightly coiled young leaf. As the stalk grows longer the fiddlehead grows larger and eventually begins to uncoil. Tree ferns of the warm rain forests of New Zealand, Australia, and Brazil that often grow to a height of 80 feet have huge brown fiddleheads at the tips of the new stalks that spring from the top of the trunk.

The sporangia on the underside of the fern leaflets have an ingenious device invented by nature to make certain the protective membranous capsule covering them bursts at the proper time and releases the spores. If a sporangium is carefully removed from the leaflet to which it clings, mounted in a drop or two of glycerine on a slide, and then examined under the low-power objective of a microscope, the image seen through the eyepiece bears some resemblance to a tennis racket. The spores are the individual cells clustered in the central part of the sporangium. Around them is the protective sporangium membrane which contains a row of specialized cells called the *annulus*. When the spores are mature it and the rest of the sporangium wall are under great tension. Then the wall breaks and the annulus flips back and forth, throwing spores in all directions. The action is similar to that which occurs when the seed pods of leguminous plants like Scotch broom and peas break and throw out their seeds when they are mature. If you examine sporangia under a microscope it is quite possible you will see this action demonstrated by some that are ready to break. Air currents will carry some of the released spores a considerable distance from the fern that produced them. This explains the presence of ferns growing in moss patches on tree trunks and branches in forests where rainfall is heavy and

Fiddleheads are the leaf buds of ferns that are pushed up through the soil in most species in early spring. They develop and unfurl to form a leaf. These are the fiddleheads of the tree fern native to some tropical countries. They grow out from the top of the upright stem or trunk.

winters are mild. Airborne spores had lodged in the moist moss and debris and, finding conditions favorable for growth, developed into ferns.

The reproductive cycle of ferns is an interesting one. It consists of two distinctly different generations—the typical fern (the *sporophyte*) and a tiny flat heart-shaped plant seldom more than a third of an inch in diameter which is called a *prothallium* (the *gametophyte*). As the prothallium develops from the spore, rootlets form on its underside and, above them, the parts which produce sperm cells. Above these are the tiny organs in which the egg cells develop. When both the eggs and the sperm cells are mature, a sperm must combine with an egg at just the right

Ferns growing in Percy's Reserve, Lower Hut, Wellington Province, New Zealand.

time if a sporophyte that will develop into a fern is to be formed.
To bring about this union there must be enough water on the prothallium to permit the sperm to reach the egg cell. This is provided by drops of rain or dew. This type of life history in which a spore-bearing plant alternates with a plant that produces egg cells and sperm cells is known as *alternation of generations.*

A great variety of ferns grow throughout most parts of North America. The filmy fern family includes a number of species that are common in tropical regions. They are relatively small and have fronds that are extremely delicate since the tissues of parts of some of the fronds consist of a single layer of cells. Ferns of this family are exported to countries in temperate regions where they are in great demand as house plants. A few species thrive in the southeastern part of the United States from Florida northward through Georgia and the Carolinas. A creeping variety finds conditions favorable along the Gulf Coast, particularly in Alabama. They flourish on cliffsides where dripping soil water gives them the moisture they require.

In botanical gardens and conservatories a number of species of ferns that are extremely interesting make excellent subjects for your camera. One of the most unusual of this group of plants is an epiphyte that is native to New Zealand called the staghorn fern. It grows on the trunks of trees in tropical and semitropical jungles. Since it cannot develop roots like other kinds of ferns, its basal leaves are modified to take over the work usually performed by a root system. These leaves overlap to form a collarlike structure that clings to the surface of its support and also forms a receptacle to hold water and decaying bits of organic matter which drain down the surface of the tree trunk. They are matted together to create a rounded portion which somewhat resembles in form the plunger used to free plumbing of anything that prevents the flow of water. All the leaves of the staghorn fern are a very pale green, tonguelike in shape, and quite long. They are not compound leaves divided into leaflets like the fronds of most of the species with which we are familiar.

Tree ferns are most abundant and attain their greatest height in certain areas of Australia, New Zealand, Hawaii, Brazil, Ceylon, and parts of both Central and South America. On this

The staghorn fern, growing in tropical and semitropical rain forests of New Zealand, Australia, New Guinea, and other parts of the world, is an epiphyte with modified leaves.

PLATYCERIUM BIFURCATUM
Staghorn Fern
Epi.Australia & New Guinea.

continent they are grown in parks and botanical gardens where conditions are favorable. Near the ocean beach in Golden Gate Park in San Francisco there is a small plot where fog sweeping shoreward from the sea during late afternoon and the warmth of California sunshine earlier in the day have created a perfect environment for the growth of tree ferns. The stands of these giant ferns attract visitors to the park.

By selecting small specimens of fronds of ferns that are native to the region in which you live and carefully drying and mounting them, beautiful specimens can be added to your leaf collection. The fronds must adhere well to the mount to prevent the possibility of dry fragile leaflets being damaged when the mounted specimens are handled. Plants like the staghorn fern from which leaf specimens cannot be taken can, of course, be photographed.

research and
10 recent discoveries

Research in recent years has solved innumerable problems pertaining to activities within plants and the ways in which they can be controlled—problems that have confronted botanists and biochemists for a long time. Increased knowledge of hormones and the role a leaf plays in the life of a plant has shattered many early explanations of plant behavior and outmoded many theories. New techniques for exploring chemical changes and examining tissue structure have been developed. The invention of the electron microscope and the use of paper chromatography to obtain information about chemical processes and composition were innovations that helped scientists probe deeper into the mysteries of the plant world. These developments and others since the end of the nineteenth century have marked the dawn of a new era in botany and related sciences. Exploring the world of plant life is no longer limited to a study of plant classification and identification.

Today, in modern research laboratories, scientists make major discoveries that can revolutionize agriculture, develop new procedures for the conservation of natural resources, and find new uses for plants and the materials that can be derived from them. The sudden realization that in the not-too-distant future ways must be provided to increase food production to prevent widespread hunger has spurred researchers to intensify their efforts to forestall such a crisis. Photosynthesis, food storage, growth, and the effect of the environment on plants have been high on the agenda for intensive investigation. The leaf as a water-waster and how water loss can be controlled is receiving much attention from men of science. The tempo of such research is particularly high in regions where water must be brought through tunnels under mountain ranges or by canals extending hundreds of miles to irrigate croplands as in the American Southwest and states like Colorado and Utah. How to increase photosynthesis and thereby add to our food supply has been a major subject of study for teams of researchers in recent years. Is there a peak above which the leaves of green plants cannot be induced to increase the amounts of sugars and starches they produce? Scientists are making intensive studies to find the answer. They are also exploring the world of plants to learn if there are species that are potential food-producers which have been overlooked in the past. Scientists sometimes originate their research projects by investigating details that, to those who are not scientific-minded, might seem to be a waste of effort, time, and money. Many projects of this kind, however, eventually lead to major discoveries that are extremely valuable. Research aimed at solving what might appear to be an insignificant problem often provides the clues that give scientists the solution to an entirely different problem of major importance.

A discovery made by Japanese scientists in 1936 led to some very enlightening studies about influencing the growth of leaves and stems. They found an unexpected source of a hormone that could change markedly the size of leaf blades and the length of stems if very dilute solutions of it were used as sprays. The investigation that led to this discovery was an attempt to find the cause of a strange plant disease which had become a serious problem in the rice paddies of Japan. For some unknown reason a high percentage of the rice that was planted yielded plants that were abnormally tall. This excessive growth drastically reduced the amount of rice produced by the plants. From the standpoint of the economy and the Japanese farmer the disease was proving disastrous. E. Kurosawa, a Japanese scientist, found that *Gibberella fujikuroi,* a fungus that had invaded the rice paddies, was responsible. From the culture in which he grew some of the fungus in his laboratory he obtained a liquid free of the parasite and sprayed it on some of the rice plants that did not have the disease. They began to grow tall stems and large leaves just like the sick plants in the fields from which the fungus had been taken and they produced very little rice. A couple of years later two other Japanese scientists separated the substance responsible for this abnormal behavior from the filtrate of the culture in which the fungus had been grown. By careful research they learned the chemical structure of the molecule of the growth-promoting hormone. Later, several more closely related compounds were discovered. The molecules of each had a structural pattern similar to the first. All were hormones—substances produced in the fungus or plant and carried to other parts of the plant body to influence growth or control the rate of some other vital activity. Their effect was very noticeable on dwarf varieties of many kinds of plants and especially on the leaves of monocots.

The gibberellin hormones have since been studied extensively to learn their effect on crops of economic value. S. H. Wittwer and M. J. Bukovac of Michigan State University cite many examples in their reports on the influence of the gibberellins on various crops. When they were sprayed on celery plants they expanded the leaf blades and increased greatly the size of the petiole which produced a remarkable increase in the yield of celery. Their effect on grasses was the same. This may be of great importance to farmers wishing to produce a lush growth on grasslands where their cattle graze or where hay is to be harvested. The gibberellins also proved very effective when sprayed on rhubarb plants. Since in both celery and rhubarb the leaf petiole is the part of the plant which is marketed, this meant a considerable increase in the yield per acre for truck farmers. A wide variety of plants, such as herbs, succulents, forest trees, and shade trees, have been treated with gibberellins. The response in most of them has been larger leaves and longer stems. Gibberellic acid is one of the most effective of this group of hormones. Extremely weak solutions are required. Less than a gram in solution is all that is needed for a whole acre of plants in many cases; others require more, possibly a few ounces of the substance per acre. The solution of the hormone is usually sprayed on the leaves. It can, however, be applied to the seeds at the time of planting in some crops. The effect will be evident in all parts of each of the plants sprayed.

Research on hormone growth-promoters began in earnest in the nineteenth century. Charles Darwin thought specific sub-

The effect of weekly applications of one of the gibberellins on cabbage plants is the growth of very large leaves and stems that are exceptionally long. The control plants are on the left; gibberellin-treated plants are on the right.

stances were created in a plant to control its growth. Similar observations were made by Julius von Sachs (1832–1897) during experiments he carried out. They led him to believe there were substances originating in the leaves that could be distributed to other parts of a plant to regulate growth. The term *hormone* had not been coined in Sachs's time. In the years since, plant hormones have attracted the attention of research scientists to an ever-increasing degree. The auxins, like the gibberellins, are hormones. They were the center of attention for a considerable time and still figure prominently in research in which the goal is to find a means of controlling plant activity. Some biochemists class gibberellins as auxins; others, because of the structural differences between the molecules and the chemical behavior of the two substances, do not group them together.

Scientists first became interested in the auxins when they worked with the tubular leaf or sheath that surrounds the primary leaves of young plants of the grasses and the grain-producers. Auxins are produced in the tip of the sheath, which is called a *coleoptile*. In other kinds of plants they are produced in the bud at the tip of the main stem. From this point they work down to other parts of the plant to either stimulate or inhibit growth. One of the auxins that is involved in this type of growth control is known chemically as indole-3-acetic acid. When it works downward in a plant it slows the growth of lateral buds. This hormone was first isolated in 1928 by a Holland-born scientist, F. W. Went (1903–   ).

The study of auxins has led to an interesting development. Sprays having different concentrations of these hormones affect growth in different ways. Very weak solutions tend to stimulate growth. Solutions with a much higher concentration of the hormone act like a poison. The amount a plant will absorb in a spraying operation also depends upon the area of the leaf blade that is characteristic of the species of plant. Lawns and pastures have been greatly improved by the use of sprays containing certain auxins. Grasses can endure a fairly high concentration of some auxins with no ill effect, but any weeds that grow with them in a lawn are poisoned by the spray since most of them have broader leaf blades. This is the reason for the effectiveness of most of the weed killers that have come into use in recent years.

Phytochrome, a pigment found in small amounts in plants, has been subjected to considerable scientific investigation in recent years. In one form it absorbs the red rays of white light and in another form, the far red or infrared rays. It is thought that phytochrome has a role in the movement of the leaf petiole. It helps the petiole to move leaves out of dark shadows and into bright sunlight. It is believed that this pigment is responsible for creating leaf mosaics, which are leaf arrangements which eliminate as far as possible the shading of leaves by others above them on the plant. The sleep-movement of leaves, petals, and sepals of flowers was studied. This phenomenon is particularly noticeable in the leaves of certain species of legumes which tend to fold up when light wanes at sundown and open up around dawn. Scientists believe that phytochrome has a major role in sleep-movement. The pigment was first isolated in the pure form in 1967.

Although there are still details and mysteries to be solved about photosynthesis, intensive research has brought to light many facts which were unknown before the 1960s. In probing the process of photosynthesis researchers have usually experimented with single-celled plants that belong to the algae division of the plant kingdom. *Chlorella* and *Scenedesmus* are genera of unicellular algae that have quite commonly been used. What takes place in these simple forms of green plant life in the way of chemical changes also occurs in the food-making mesophyll tissues of the leaf of a maple, cabbage, or any other green plant. Dr. Melvin Calvin of the University of California and his co-workers used both of these algae in their investigations of the intermediate chemical reactions that occur in the interval between the striking of a light photon and its capture by a molecule of chlorophyll and the moment that a molecule of glucose is produced. Both paper chromatography and the use of a radioactive isotope of carbon, C^{14}, in the compound $C^{14}O_2$ were employed to permit the tracing of the course of a chemical change. The resulting achievement of discovering the complex series of reactions that occurs won for Dr. Calvin the Nobel prize in 1961.

Until quite recently *Chlorella* was the subject of intensive study in the research laboratories of some of the principal universities of Japan for another reason. It was looked upon as a possible source of food that could be used when increased population in the world might force man to use foods he is not accustomed to using today. *Chlorella* was grown in large tanks and pools. It was generally agreed that the growing of *Chlorella* in vast quantities is feasible, but that, at the present time, it could not compete with foods readily available and more popular with consumers.

Transpiration and how to reduce it has loomed large in the mind of many a scientist because this activity of leaves and its relation to the water table in the soil of many regions is of major importance. Exploring the behavior of the guard cells that flank the micropores of leaf surfaces and the ways of controlling them to reduce the wasting of water is an important problem today. The control of transpiration is looked upon as one of the ways of preventing a food crisis in the world of tomorrow. At the Connecticut Agricultural Experiment Station extensive studies of transpiration have been made during the past several years. The studies were initiated by a program of testing the transpiration rate of small trees in the laboratories and greenhouses of the station before and after spraying them with certain chemicals. They were substances which, when they are absorbed, reduce the size of the pores through which water vapor escapes. Such antitranspirants produced no ill effects in the plants. Also, by reducing the amount of water loss, they did not deprive the plants of the water they need for growth or other normal activities. Plants usually absorb about nine times as much water as they need and transpire the rest into the atmosphere. The next step was to spray large plots of forest. The spraying was done near the start of the summer season and, in later tests, in midsummer. Periodic tests were made of the amount of moisture in the soil and the results were gratifying. They indicated that from twenty to thirty thousand gallons of water per acre accumulated above the quantity held in the soil in other areas where spraying had not been done. The decrease in the size of the pores (stomata) in the leaves was measured by an instrument known as a porometer. Neil C. Turner, reporting on the progress made in this research program, explains that the reduction in water loss from the soil and the prevention of severe drought during the summer were ample rewards for the years of patient research the program required.

These are just a few examples of what research has accomplished. Scientists in many of the agricultural experiment stations of the various states and in the national laboratories of

the United States Department of Agriculture and other government agencies are constantly probing for the solutions to
problems pertaining to plants. A layman might see little of
value in a scientist devoting his time to comparing the shades of
green and yellow in the colors of the leaves of tobacco plants.
Equally puzzling would be the hours that a research scientist
might spend smearing leaves with Vaseline to determine the
rates of carbon dioxide and oxygen absorption of the cuticle and
the stomata. Investigations like these, however, often give clues
that will start a team of scientists on the path to a major
discovery.

There are many problems still to be solved about leaves and

Coconut palms fringe the shore of the island of Tobago in the West Indies. The crown of leaves tops the long slender trunk. Leaves of the coconut palm have long been used as thatch by the inhabitants of Tobago and other tropical islands when building the roof of a hut.

how they serve the plant. The future will bring many more. The need for research will always be with us. Young people of today with an interest in plant life and the environment who have explored some of the fields of botanical science, collected leaves, gathered specimens for a herbarium of their own, and gone into the countryside to learn how plants live will find they have chosen a fascinating hobby. Some will become so enthusiastic they will make it a life project and become the scientists who will probe for solutions to the problems pertaining to leaves and plants that confront man in the world of tomorrow.

All photographs were taken by the author except for those indicated below, and for which the author makes grateful acknowledgment.

Pages 97, 98, 101: Crown copyright; reproduced with permission of the Controller of Her Majesty's Stationery Office and the Director, Royal Botanic Gardens, Kew, England.

Page 42: Information Division, Radiation Laboratory, University of California, Berkeley, California.

Page 126: New Zealand Government Travel Commission.

Page 94: South African Tourist Corporation.

Pages 65, 66: Dr. Elliot Weier, Professor of Botany, University of California, Davis, California.

Page 37: Dr. J. S. C. Wessels, Philips Research Laboratories, Eindhoven, Netherlands.

Page 134: S. H. Wittwer, Director, Michigan Agricultural Experiment Station.

index

about the author

Raymond A. Wohlrabe is a well-known science and travel writer. Having taught science in high school for many years, he became interested in making use of his experiences in writing books that would be popular with young people. He has written on crystals, electrostatics, solar energy, and giant molecules, and in his books includes experiments that were tried out in his own classes. His great knowledge of photography and his extensive travels are also reflected in many books and articles.

Mr. Wohlrabe took most of the beautiful pictures that illustrate this present book. He received the Governor's Award in Olympia, Washington, for his writings; he himself lives in Seattle.

about the illustrator

John F. McTarsney, who did the diagrams, is a commercial artist specializing in the fields of advertising and of designing audiovisual aids. He lives and works in Staten Island, where he has his studio, in the same area that members of his family have lived since 1837.